Tourism: An International Approach

Tourism: An International Approach

Francisco Peralta

Willford Press
www.willfordpress.com

Published by Willford Press,
118-35 Queens Blvd., Suite 400,
Forest Hills, NY 11375, USA

ISBN: 978-1-64728-375-9

Cataloging-in-Publication Data

Tourism : an international approach / Francisco Peralta.
p. cm.
Includes bibliographical references and index.
ISBN 978-1-64728-375-9
1. Tourism. 2. Travel. 3. Service industries. 4. Hospitality industry. I. Peralta, Francisco.
G155.A1 T68 2021
338.479 1--dc23

For information on all Willford Press publications
visit our website at www.willfordpress.com

Willford Press

Table of Contents

Preface

This book aims to help a broader range of students by exploring a wide variety of significant topics related to this discipline. It will help students in achieving a higher level of understanding of the subject and excel in their respective fields. This book would not have been possible without the unwavered support of my senior professors who took out the time to provide me feedback and help me with the process. I would also like to thank my family for their patience and support.

Traveling for recreational purposes is known as tourism. There can be two types of tourisms - international and national tourism. International tourism has both incoming and outgoing effects on a country's balance of payments. It has become an important source of income for many countries. International tourism is an essential activity that affects the social, educational, cultural and economic sectors of countries as well as influences their international relations. Mass tourism and niche tourism are the two forms of international tourism. Mass tourism refers to the traveling done by groups on pre-scheduled tours under the organization of tourism professionals. The central feature of mass tourism is the relationship between transportation operators, tourism companies and hotels. Niche tourism refers to various specialty forms of tourism such as agritourism, culinary tourism, dark tourism, heritage tourism, extreme tourism, film tourism and wildlife tourism. This book provides comprehensive insights into international tourism. It picks up individual branches and explains their need and contribution in the context of a growing economy. It will serve as a valuable source of reference for those interested in this field.

A brief overview of the book contents is provided below:

Chapter - Introduction

Tourism between international borders is referred to as international tourism. It is considered as a global leisure activity that helps in acquirement of knowledge and experience. This is an introductory chapter which will briefly introduce all the significant aspects of international tourism as well as its merits and demerits.

Chapter - Types of International Tourism

There are numerous types of international tourism. These include religious tourism, international volunteering, ecotourism, niche tourism, city tourism, enotourism, business tourism, sports tourism, culinary tourism, extreme tourism, mass tourism, craft beer tourism, etc. This chapter has been carefully written to provide an easy understanding of the various kinds of international tourisms.

Chapter - Cultural Tourism

Tourism that aims to explore the cultural aspects of any region comes under cultural tourism. Some of the example include archaeological tourism, holocaust tourism, dracula tourism, heritage tourism, music tourism, pop-culture tourism, literary tourism, etc. The topics elaborated in this chapter will help in gaining a better perspective about different types of cultural tourism.

Chapter – Medical Tourism

People traveling abroad in order to get medical treatment, is called medical tourism. It generally takes from less-developed countries, not having enough medical facilities, to developed countries. Wellness tourism, fertility tourism and dental tourism are some examples of it. All these diverse medical tourisms have been carefully analyzed in this chapter.

Chapter – Adventure Tourism

The type of tourism involving exploration of places or travelling to remote areas, in order to experience the thrill of surroundings, is referred to as adventure tourism. It covers hot air ballooning, zip lining, free falling, rafting, spelunking, mountaineering, etc. This chapter has been carefully written to provide an in-depth knowledge of various kinds of adventure tourism.

Chapter – Components of Tourism and Travel Industry

Tourism is a vast domain comprising of several components that facilitate it. These are tourism transportation, travel agency, tourist attraction, tour operator, travel agency, etc. The topics elaborated in this chapter will help in gaining a better perspective about all the components of tourism and travel industry.

Chapter – Tourism: Activities and Accomodations

Activities such as trekking, mountaineering, rafting, paragliding, walking tour, etc. come under tourism activities. Guest ranch, holiday cottage, home exchange, etc. are some examples of tourist accommodations. This chapter closely examines activities and accommodations of tourism to provide an extensive understanding of the subject.

Chapter – Technological Aspects of Tourism

There are a number of technological provisions that aid tourists. Electronic ticket, flight tracking, biometric passport, online hotel reservations, mobile ticketing, audio tour, virtual tour, global distribution system are some of the provisions that fall in this domain. All these diverse technological aspects of tourism have been carefully analyzed in this chapter.

Francisco Peralta

1

Introduction

Tourism between international borders is referred to as international tourism. It is considered as a global leisure activity that helps in acquirement of knowledge and experience. This is an introductory chapter which will briefly introduce all the significant aspects of international tourism as well as its merits and demerits.

Tourism

Tourism is the act and process of spending time away from home in pursuit of recreation, relaxation, and pleasure, while making use of the commercial provision of services. As such, tourism is a product of modern social arrangements, beginning in western Europe in the 17th century, although it has antecedents in Classical antiquity. It is distinguished from exploration in that tourists follow a "beaten path," benefit from established systems of provision, and, as befits pleasure-seekers, are generally insulated from difficulty, danger, and embarrassment. Tourism, however, overlaps with other activities, interests, and processes, including, for example, pilgrimage. This gives rise to shared categories, such as "business tourism," "sports tourism," and "medical tourism" (international travel undertaken for the purpose of receiving medical care).

By the early 21st century, international tourism had become one of the world's most important economic activities, and its impact was becoming increasingly apparent from the Arctic to Antarctica. The history of tourism is therefore of great interest and importance. That history begins long before the coinage of the word tourist at the end of the 18th century. In the Western tradition, organized travel with supporting infrastructure, sightseeing, and an emphasis on essential destinations and experiences can be found in ancient Greece and Rome, which can lay claim to the origins of both "heritage tourism" (aimed at the celebration and appreciation of historic sites of recognized cultural importance) and beach resorts. The Seven Wonders of the World became tourist sites for Greeks and Romans.

Monk standing at the Kyaiktiyo (Golden Rock) pagoda, a historic Buddhist pilgrimage destination in eastern Myanmar (Burma).

Hindu pilgrims bathing in the Ganges River at Varanasi, Uttar Pradesh state, India.

Pilgrimage offers similar antecedents, bringing Eastern civilizations into play. Its religious goals coexist with defined routes, commercial hospitality, and an admixture of curiosity, adventure, and enjoyment among the motives of the participants. Pilgrimage to the earliest Buddhist sites began more than 2,000 years ago, although it is hard to define a transition from the makeshift privations of small groups of monks to recognizably tourist practices. Pilgrimage to Mecca is of similar antiquity. The tourist status of the hajj is problematic given the number of casualties that even in the 21st century continued to be suffered on the journey through the desert. The thermal spa as a tourist destination regardless of the pilgrimage associations with the site as a holy well or sacred spring is not necessarily a European invention, despite deriving its English-language label from Spa, an early resort in what is now Belgium. The oldest Japanese onsen (hot springs) were catering to bathers from at least the 6th century. Tourism has been a global phenomenon from its origins.

Modern tourism is an increasingly intensive, commercially organized, business-oriented set of activities whose roots can be found in the industrial and postindustrial West. The aristocratic grand tour of cultural sites in France, Germany, and especially Italy including those associated with Classical Roman tourism had its roots in the 16th century. It grew rapidly, however, expanding its geographical range to embrace Alpine scenery during the second half of the 18th century, in the intervals between European wars. (If truth is historically the first casualty of war, tourism is the second, although it may subsequently incorporate pilgrimages to graves and battlefield sites and even, by the late 20th century, to concentration camps.) As part of the grand tour's expansion, its exclusivity was undermined as the expanding commercial, professional, and industrial middle ranks joined the landowning and political classes in aspiring to gain access to this rite of passage for their sons. By the early 19th century, European journeys for health, leisure, and culture became common practice among the middle classes, and paths to the acquisition of cultural capital (that array of knowledge, experience, and polish that was necessary to mix in polite society) were smoothed by guidebooks, primers, the development of art and souvenir markets, and carefully calibrated transport and accommodation systems.

Transport innovation was an essential enabler of tourism's spread and democratization and its ultimate globalization. Beginning in the mid-19th century, the steamship and the railway brought greater comfort and speed and cheaper travel, in part because fewer overnight and intermediate stops were needed. Above all else, these innovations allowed for reliable time-tabling, essential for those who were tied to the discipline of the calendar if not the clock. The gaps in accessibility to these transport systems were steadily closing in the later 19th century, while the empire of steam was becoming global. Railways promoted domestic as well as international tourism, including short visits to the coast, city, and countryside which might last less than a day but fell clearly into the "tourism" category. Rail travel also made grand tour destinations more widely accessible, reinforcing existing tourism flows while contributing to tensions and clashes between classes and cultures among the tourists. By the late 19th century, steam navigation and railways were opening tourist destinations from Lapland to New Zealand, and the latter opened the first dedicated national tourist office in 1901.

After World War II, governments became interested in tourism as an invisible import and as a tool of diplomacy, but prior to this time international travel agencies took the lead in easing the complexities of tourist journeys. The most famous of these agencies was Britain's Thomas Cook and Son organization, whose operations spread from Europe and the Middle East across the globe in the late 19th century. The role played by other firms (including the British tour organizers Frame's and Henry Gaze and Sons) has been less visible to 21st-century observers, not least because these agencies did not preserve their records, but they were equally important. Shipping lines also promoted international tourism from the late 19th century onward. From the Norwegian fjords to the Caribbean, the pleasure cruise was already becoming a distinctive tourist experience before World War I, and transatlantic companies competed for middle-class tourism during the 1920s and '30s. Between the World Wars, affluent Americans journeyed by air and sea to a variety of destinations in the Caribbean and Latin America.

Tourism became even bigger business internationally in the latter half of the 20th century as air travel was progressively deregulated and decoupled from "flag carriers" (national airlines). The airborne package tour to sunny coastal destinations became the basis of an enormous annual migration from northern Europe to the Mediterranean before extending to a growing variety of long-haul destinations, including Asian markets in the Pacific, and eventually bringing postcommunist Russians and eastern Europeans to the Mediterranean. Similar traffic flows expanded from the United States to Mexico and the Caribbean. In each case these developments built on older rail-, road-, and sea-travel patterns. The earliest package tours to the Mediterranean were by motor coach (bus) during the 1930s and postwar years. It was not until the late 1970s that Mediterranean sun and sea vacations became popular among working-class families in northern Europe; the label "mass tourism," which is often applied to this phenomenon, is misleading. Such holidays were experienced in a variety of ways because tourists had choices, and the destination resorts varied widely in history, culture, architecture, and visitor mix. From the 1990s the growth of flexible international travel through the rise of budget airlines, notably easyJet and Ryanair in Europe, opened a new mix of destinations. Some of these were former Soviet-bloc locales such as Prague and Riga, which appealed to weekend and short-break European tourists who constructed their own itineraries in negotiation with local service providers, mediated through the airlines' special deals. In international tourism, globalization has not been a one-way process; it has entailed negotiation between hosts and guests.

Day-trippers and Domestic Tourism

Tourists in yellow raincoats observing Niagara Falls, Ontario, Canada.

While domestic tourism could be seen as less glamorous and dramatic than international traffic flows, it has been more important to more people over a longer period. From the 1920s the rise of Florida as a destination for American tourists has been characterized by "snowbirds" from the northern and Midwestern states traveling a greater distance across the vast expanse of the United States than many European tourists travel internationally. Key phases in the pioneering development of tourism as a commercial phenomenon in Britain were driven by domestic demand and local journeys. European wars in the late 18th and early 19th centuries prompted the "discovery of Britain" and the rise of the Lake District and Scottish Highlands as destinations for both the upper classes and the aspiring classes. The railways helped to open the seaside to working-class day-trippers and holidaymakers, especially in the last quarter of the 19th century. By 1914 Blackpool in Lancashire, the world's first working-class seaside resort, had around four million visitors per summer. Coney Island in Brooklyn, New York, had more visitors by this time, but most were day-trippers who came from and returned to locations elsewhere in the New York City area by train the same day. Domestic tourism is less visible in statistical terms and tends to be serviced by regional, local, and small family-run enterprises. The World Tourism Organization, which tries to count tourists globally, is more concerned with the international scene, but across the globe, and perhaps especially in Asia, domestic tourism remains much more important in numerical terms than the international version.

Coney Island: Luna Park, Luna Park, Coney Island.

International Tourism

An international tourist crosses the boundaries of many countries, uses different currencies, faces different languages and meets different types of people. Usually international tourism involves longer distances although crossing small countries or travelling in the neighbourhood of international borders may involve short distances.

International Tourism and Number of Arrivals

International inbound tourists (overnight visitors) are the number of tourists who travel to a country other than that in which they have their usual residence, but outside their usual environment, for a period not exceeding 12 months and whose main purpose in visiting is other than an activity remunerated from within the country visited. When data on number of tourists are not available, the number of visitors, which includes tourists, same-day visitors, cruise passengers, and crew members, is shown instead. Sources and collection methods for arrivals differ across countries. In some cases data are from border statistics (police, immigration, and the like) and supplemented by border surveys. In other cases data are from tourism accommodation establishments. For some countries number of arrivals is limited to arrivals by air and for others to arrivals staying in hotels. Some countries include arrivals of nationals residing abroad while others do not. Caution should thus be used in comparing arrivals across countries. The data on inbound tourists refer to the number of arrivals, not to the number of people traveling. Thus a person who makes several trips to a country during a given period is counted each time as a new arrival.

The map below shows how International tourism, number of arrivals varies by country. The shade of the country corresponds to the magnitude of the indicator. The darker the shade, the higher the value. The country with the highest value in the world is France, with a value of 84,452,000.00. The country with the lowest value in the world is Tuvalu, with a value of 2,400.00.

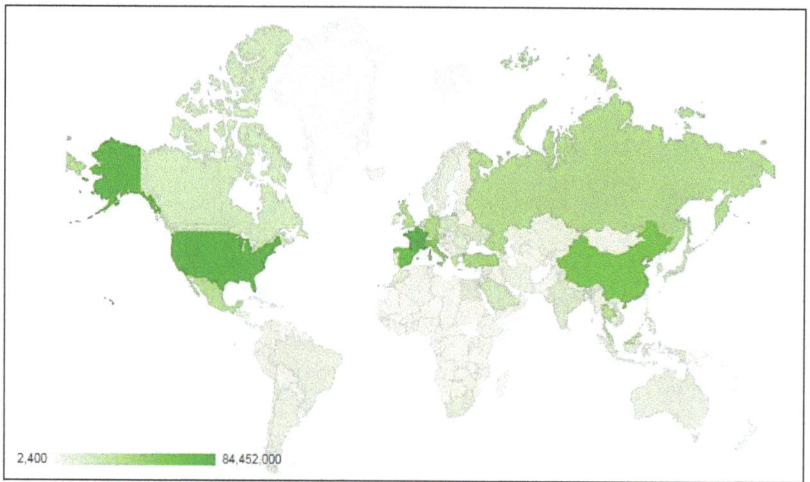

Development Relevance: Tourism is officially recognized as a directly measurable activity, enabling more accurate analysis and more effective policy. Whereas previously the sector relied mostly on approximations from related areas of measurement (e.g. Balance of Payments statistics), tourism today possesses a range of instruments to track its productive activities and the activities of the consumers that drive them: visitors (both tourists and excursionists). An increasing number of countries have opened up and invested in tourism development, making tourism a key driver of socio-economic progress through export revenues, the creation of jobs and enterprises, and infrastructure development. As an internationally traded service, inbound tourism has become one of the world's major trade categories. For many developing countries it is one of the main sources of foreign exchange income and a major component of exports, creating much needed employment and development opportunities.

Limitations and Exceptions: Tourism can be either domestic or international. The data refers to international tourism, where the traveler's country of residence differs from the visiting country. International tourism consists of inbound (arrival) and outbound (departures) tourism. The data are from the World Tourism Organization (WTO), a United Nations agency. The data on inbound and outbound tourists refer to the number of arrivals and departures, not to the number of people traveling. Thus a person who makes several trips to a country during a given period is counted each time as a new arrival. The data on inbound tourism show the arrivals of nonresident tourists (overnight visitors) at national borders. When data on international tourists are unavailable or incomplete, the data show the arrivals of international visitors, which include tourists, same-day visitors, cruise passengers, and crew members. Sources and collection methods for arrivals differ across countries. In some cases data are from border statistics (police, immigration, and the like) and supplemented by border surveys. In other cases data are from tourism accommodation establishments. For some countries number of arrivals is limited to arrivals by air and for others to arrivals staying in hotels. Some countries include arrivals of nationals residing abroad while others do not. Caution should thus be used in comparing arrivals across countries.

Statistical Concept and Methodology: Statistical information on tourism is based mainly on data on arrivals and overnight stays along with balance of payments information. These data do not completely capture the economic phenomenon of tourism or provide the information needed for effective public policies and efficient business operations. Data are needed on the scale and significance of tourism. Information on the role of tourism in national economies is particularly deficient. Although the World Tourism Organization reports progress in harmonizing definitions and measurement, differences in national practices still prevent full comparability. Arrivals data measure the flows of international visitors to the country of reference: each arrival corresponds to one in inbound tourism trip. If a person visits several countries during the course of a single trip, his/her arrival in each country is recorded separately. In an accounting period, arrivals are not necessarily equal to the number of persons travelling (when a person visits the same country several times a year, each trip by the same person is counted as a separate arrival). Arrivals data should correspond to inbound visitors by including both tourists and same-day non-resident visitors. All other types of travelers (such as border, seasonal and other short-term workers, long-term students and others) should be excluded as they do not qualify as visitors. Data are obtained from different sources: administrative records (immigration, traffic counts, and other possible types of controls), border surveys or a mix of them. If data are obtained from accommodation surveys, the number of guests is used as estimate of arrival figures; consequently, in this case, breakdowns by regions, main purpose of the trip, modes of transport used or forms of organization of the trip are based on complementary visitor surveys.

Positive and Negative Effects of Tourism

Travel and tourism is one of the world's largest industries. It "surpasses that of oil exports, food products or automobiles," according to the United Nations World Tourism Organization. Inbound tourism boosts the economic growth of a region's economy while providing high potential to support job creation. Outbound tourism promotes cross-cultural understanding and goodwill. In the words of Mark Twain, "Travel is fatal to prejudice, bigotry, and narrow-mindedness."

Positive Economic Effects of Tourism

Job creation is paramount to any discussion about tourism's positive economic effects. The 2017 Economic Impact Report by the World Travel & Tourism Council indicates that the industry generates one out of 10 jobs worldwide, growing at a pace that outperforms employment in the global economy for the sixth consecutive year. The report also indicates that among new jobs, the sector accounts for one in five.

Positive Environmental Effects of Tourism

Education about the reasons for sustainable tourism places a spotlight on responsible planning. As more consumers become aware of the lasting benefits of "take only pictures, leave only footprints," we can better respect nature and minimize the impact on any habitat we visit.

Positive Effects of Mega Events

A rotating mega event, such as the Olympics, the World Cup or even a pop-up happening such as a high profile royal wedding, will benefit a host destination by attracting global attention. Large numbers of spectators visit, injecting significant cash into the local economy. International sporting events also serve as catalysts for longer term improvements in stadiums, facilities, transportation and infrastructures. For Athens, Greece, in 2004 and for Pyeongchang, South Korea, in 2018, this even meant new airport terminals.

Positive Social Effects of Tourism

Tourism has long been cited by world leaders as a driver of peace and security through understanding. In the 21st century, tourism is closely linked to development, embracing a growing number of new destinations – hence new jobs. Tourism can create civic pride by encouraging cultivation and sharing of local customs, food, traditions and festivals. Personal exchanges between hosts and guests goes a long way toward fostering better cultural understanding. Tour operators are focusing on the experiential travel trend, providing more authentic and immersive experiences for their guests. Open spaces and national parks in countries around the world are good for replenishing both body and soul, but traffic jams are not a good look.

Negative Economic Effects of Tourism

Unexpected and unforeseeable events such as terrorism, political upheaval, impactful weather conditions and natural disasters can wreak havoc on a region, negatively affecting inbound tourism for considerable periods of time. The more dependent a destination is on tourism, the more the impact will be felt and the longer recovery will take.

Negative Environmental Effects of Tourism

Too many tourists can have a negative impact on the quality of life. Known as overtourism, this phenomenon is creating a burden in such destinations as rural Patagonia, Chile, and urban Barcelona, Spain. The slopes of Mount Everest are littered and, in Iceland, tourists far outnumber the resident population. In the U.S. where the top 10 parks saw more than 44 million visitors in 2016, the National Park Service is looking for ways to protect natural treasures in light of year-on-year increases in visitor numbers.

Negative Effects of Mega Events

Those rows of empty arena seats at the London 2012 Olympics have been attributed to the toxic fear of crowds, disruption and ultra high prices that served to block intentions of locals and travelers. We've all observed that the legacy left by hosting a major event can hurt a local economy more than it benefits. In years following the 2004 Olympic Games in Athens, venues went unused although the city chalked up a $15 billion price tag. Four years later, the same thing happened at the far more costly Beijing Olympics. During the 2013 America's Cup, "equal amounts of civic pride and political controversy" were generated, reported the San Francisco Chronicle, which also reported the unpaid tab for the host city was $11.5 million.

Negative Social Effects of Tourism

While tourism can help preserve cultures, it can also water them down via commercialization and cookie-cutter approaches. Airbnb's advertising has attacked the sameness of hotels, suggesting real people's homes in real neighborhoods as an alternative. There is nothing authentic about a hotel's nightly staging of an indoor Hawaiian luau featuring acrobatic fire dancers or the "Venetian" gondola that plies a fake canal on the Vegas strip in the shadow of the "Eiffel Tower." Such features have none of the social benefits that a truly genuine travel experience can produce.

2

Types of International Tourism

There are numerous types of international tourism. These include religious tourism, international volunteering, ecotourism, niche tourism, city tourism, enotourism, business tourism, sports tourism, culinary tourism, extreme tourism, mass tourism, craft beer tourism, etc. This chapter has been carefully written to provide an easy understanding of the various kinds of international tourisms.

Religious Tourism

Religious tourism is an important part of the tourism industry it called special interest tourism, which usually related to the followers of particular faiths who visit locations that are considered as holy sites.

Religious sites are not only visited by the pilgrims but also visited by non-religious tourists since they have cultural, historical and religious significance.

Most niche of tourism industry is directly affected by economic instability but this religious tourism is less affected by these economic issues because the reason for travelling is very strong and it plays a very important role in their lives so money does not play a very vital role to stop from visiting a destination.

Religious tourism is the pioneer form of tourism which has begun almost with the dawn of humanity. From the ancient times religious destinations were not only a part of the cultural landscape but they also had become a vital factor in local marketing and prime parts of the economy of hosted destinations. Some of the religious places such as Mecca in Saudi Arabia, Fatima in Portugal and Lourdes in France attract millions of religious tourists, charity workers, missionaries and humanitarians creating a huge financial transaction in the destination.

Religious tourism, in the literature of tourism studies is, often described interchangeably as a cultural heritage tourism, cultural tourism, cultural heritage tourism and spiritual tourism by different authors.

It is difficult to give a specific definition of religious tourism and the reason behind it is that cultural and religious travel are used synonymously. This is because the majority of cultural tourists visit religious destinations as a part of their itinerary and are thus referred to as religious tourists.

The general meaning of religious tourism implies travelling with the prime motive of experiencing religious activities or the products they induce such as art, culture, traditions and architecture.

Religion and tourism are interlinked with each other. The pioneer form of tourism was in the form of visiting religious pilgrimages such as Christians travelling to Jerusalem and Muslims to Mecca. Religious pilgrimages have always been one of the dominant factors for motivating people to travel. Tracing back to the religious history it is found that major religions have globally stimulated tourism as a foundation for spreading their own religious beliefs.

Marketing of Religious Products and Services

The interconnections of religion and marketing of religious products seem to be ineluctable in our culture with some striking similarities. Religious people see the religious products and services as a means of conveying their faith while sellers see them as a means of spreading faith. Religion and marketing institutions both depend on conveying a message and a willingness of people to believe in what is intellectually unbelievable. Through the means of rituals, practices and myths religions creates their meaning while marketing does the same through advertising and shopping. Similarly, religion is about accepting a belief system and marketing is accepting belief about a product. Religions have faith communities while marketing has brand communities. Religion and marketing have a symbiotic relationship, for example, religion is considered as a product and the products as religions.

International Volunteering

International volunteering is when volunteers contribute their time to work for organisations or causes outside their respective home countries. In most such cases, volunteers work in developing countries on international development programmes with local volunteer organisations that conduct activities such as health promotion, education and environmental conservation. Trends show that international volunteering has become increasingly popular across many countries over the past few decades. International volunteering is a broad term which is used to capture multi-year, skilled placements as well as short term roles, recently termed *voluntourism*, and a range of activities in between conducted by governments, charities and travel agents.

Volunteer Demographics

Global statistics on international volunteers are unavailable. However, about one million people from the US volunteer abroad each year almost half for less than two weeks. Shorter-term voluntourism is therefore appealing to many, as it is targeted at travellers who want to make a positive change in the world, while still providing a touristic experience. Volunteering appeals to a broad cross-section of society, but the majority of volunteers are in their twenties and thirties, potentially due to perceptions of volunteering abroad being a more risky activity. The average age of Voluntary Service Overseas (VSO) volunteers, however, is 38, showing a broad range of participation across age groups. Recently there has been an increase in baby boomer volunteers. One possible explanation for the increase is that these people are transitioning into a new stage of life and their focus may shift toward finding activities that give their life new meaning. As with domestic volunteering, international volunteering is more common among those with a higher education and from higher income households.

Critiques and Challenges

Certain critiques and challenges are associated with international volunteering.

Outcomes

Measuring the outcomes of international volunteering is an ongoing challenge. Sometimes the costs invested in these partnerships are high. The intangible nature of impact and outcomes is hard to measure and research has been proposed in this area. Similarly, how to measure the success of a volunteer and the supporting organisation's performance is complicated. To allow volunteers to integrate properly into the community, it is essential that volunteers have some useful skills and are reasonably well-informed and trained before the placement. Shannon O'Donnell, a vocal critic of poorly designed international programs, contends that many volunteer organizations compromise the dignity of local populations these programs often foster a cyclical dependency international volunteers within the communities the programs are designed to serve. Others have critiqued the mixing of models of volunteering designed for international understanding and those designed for social or economic development. Still others are concerned about it postcolonial and historical character, and the impacts this has on the identity of members of hosting communities.

High Costs

Related to the impact of international volunteering, the cost of having an international volunteer has been cited as another area of concern, especially costs for air tickets, allowances, insurance, training and logistics. Local staff do require such costs, and the local organisations could put these funds into more important issues; however, many volunteers pay these expenses personally. Some institutions provide scholarships for international volunteering. Still, volunteers are often cheaper than other forms of long-term technical assistance because they live and work under local conditions. Expatriates who work in the same capacity can be paid multiple times more than any allowances volunteers receive (if any). The cost-benefit of international volunteers is hard to quantify, though studies have highlighted improvements in well-being and inter-cultural understanding in communities and schools as a result of international exchanges and volunteers.

Undermining Local Organizations

One consideration is that volunteers may dominate the local workplace, replace local employment, and undermine management and work culture especially in small organisations and schools. This is due to volunteers often being considered more highly educated than local staff, even if they do not often have much direct experience. Coming from a different culture can also lead to volunteers imposing their values on organisations. On the other hand, volunteers are often trained to respect the local working culture and ethics. Also, since they report directly to local organisations, they can (and somctimes do) have their contracts terminated if they break any local regulations, which helps to reduce concerns of domination.

Low Skills and Experience

Young and unexperienced international volunteers sometimes do not have the correct skill-set to achieve their project goal. While this may be fine for volunteer workcamps and volunteer trips designed around enhancing international and intercultural understanding, it is a significant problem for international development volunteering (IDV). On the other hand, many of the most prominent international volunteer cooperation organizations (IVCOs) especially those funded by governments have minimal educational and skill requirements.

A group of volunteers during training.

Poor Understandings of Local Context

International volunteers from outside the host community can lack an understanding of the local context. While there is often a vetting or selection process for volunteers before they are recruited to serve in developing countries, this process has at times been found wanting. Large international volunteer cooperation organizations (IVCOs) provide their volunteers with significant training before and often their placement, which can help address this deficit. On the other hand, countless smaller and for-profit IVCOs offering unskilled volunteer placements to any participant willing to pay the placement fee rarely provide the type of training and preparation that volunteers need to be successful and helpful in hosting communities. In these circumstances, there is conflict about whether the fees volunteers pay justify the time spent supervising and revising their work, and if a sufficient portion of the fees make it back to the local communities hosting volunteers who are typically responsible for their supervision and training.

Neo-colonialism

There have been allegations from some quarters of neo-colonial advances disguised as an effort to tackle poverty, as some volunteer organisations are connected to national governments, e.g. the Peace Corps, which was set up by the American government. Despite this challenge, most volunteer organisations are non-governmental (NGOs) and are not influenced by government policies. The present structures of international volunteering are also often aimed at impacts on a local, community scale which is sharply in contrast with the macro-political government strategies of the colonial era.

However, many academic journals elaborate that volunteers often have little knowledge or expertise in the work they do when volunteering abroad. This has raised concerns of its value. Frances Brown and Derek Hall write that this creates a neo-colonial narrative; they say the volunteer perspective is framed around the idea that Westerners with minimal experience can effect change in the Global South, just by nature of being from the West. This perpetuates the narrative of Western domination in a post-colonial world, and the need to "save" and "help" the Global South.

Motivations of Volunteers

People volunteer for many reasons, but seldom does anyone volunteer strictly for monetary reasons, as very few organisations offer a stipend for volunteering. More compelling motives include experiencing another culture, meeting new people, and advancing one's career prospects. Such motivations are common among younger volunteers who are looking for experience or direction in their careers. People generally volunteer in order to increase their international awareness, to contextualize poverty and its effects, as an education opportunity, and to help people while having a morally rewarding experience. Many believe that the trip will change the way they think when they return home. However, others are just looking to give to others and do not believe that their experience will cause them to think twice about their lives back home. Many participants use these trips to boost their resumes, travel with friends, gain world experience, and see new countries.

A common motivation is to "make a difference" and to "achieve something positive for others" who are less fortunate than the volunteer. Many volunteers tend to concur that there are disadvantaged people in their home countries, but the scale of disadvantage outside their home countries is felt to be greater. Volunteering at home may elicit images of helping the less fortunate, or campaigning with a local pressure group. Volunteering abroad has tended to be associated with international development and bridging the divide between the rich and poor worlds. Volunteering abroad often seems a more worthy contribution in this context to the volunteers than work in their own country. This perspective is particularly true of volunteers who are older and looking for something more value-based as they near the end of their professional careers or after their children have left home.

Voluntourism

Volunteer tourism, also known as "voluntourism", is a specific kind of international volunteering. It is a relatively new concept, combining the nonprofit sector and the tourism sector. Essentially, it is a form of international traveling to resource poor settings, with a primary purpose of volunteering and serving the host community. Voluntourism activities are generally temporary attempts to address education, health, environmental and economic issues. Ideally, voluntourism activities are conducted by non-profit organizations for the purpose of societal good, and poses a chance for volunteers to help and benefit others in an unconventional setting with their skills. Those activities are characterized by the age of the participants, and by the length of time they volunteer abroad. Participants are often young adults (ages 15–30), the length of the trip is often categorized as short term (under three months), and the volunteering is regularly packaged with adventure and travel activities. Voluntourism has undergone intense scrutiny over the course of the 2000s, and an increasing number of academic papers question volunteer tourists' motivations and experiences.

Growth of Voluntourism

As a variation of international volunteering, voluntourism's development can be traced back to over a century ago. it is one of the most rapid growing trends in modern travel, with more than 1.6 million volunteer-tourists spending around two billion dollars each year.

Criticisms

Voluntourism programs are more often conducted by profit-making companies rather than charities. Although the intention for volunteers to travel is to empower the local communities, the ultimate motivation of the volunteers is more self-serving. the motivations identified by the participants generally fit under the category of personal growth (e.g. skill development, cross-cultural understanding, career choice, etc.), while motivations related to having a positive social impact or desire for social justice in the host communities was not found among the participants, reflecting a one-directional flow of benefits from the host communities to the volunteers. With this trend, communities, journalists, and those who have actually done volunteer activities start to question to which extent voluntourism activities can actually help with the local condition, or will they actually bring harm to the already underprivileged places.

Volunteer-sending organizations, have been critiqued as furthering the aforementioned neo-colonial narrative to youth. The increased prevalence of promotional material regarding trips to "help" the Global South has "increased media exposure in the Global North to poverty in the Global South." Critics argue that the way in which these organizations advertise their trips stigmatizes and frames the developing world as helpless. This plays into Maria Eriksson Baaz's theories in the book *Paternalism of Partnership: a Postcolonial Reading of Identity in Development Aid*, in which she discusses discourse that frames the volunteer as a developed, paternalistic individual and the donor as underdeveloped. The framing and "othering" of cultures outside the West and Global North can also be found in Edward Said's text, *Orientalism*. His theory is rooted in the same idea, in which he describes West's patronizing portrayals of the East.

Other criticisms of the voluntourism industry are that not only are short-term volunteers often untrained in the projects they participate in (building schools, health centres, wells), but that projects can fuel conflict among communities, offer bandaid solutions, replace work locals could be doing, and reinforce neoliberal policies. Interactions with children are highly popular amongst voluntourism programs. As a consequence, children in these communities may become dependent and commodified when volunteers are constantly arriving and departing every couple weeks. Orphanage volunteering is also an emerging program, which can fuel human trafficking or child abuse in the host communities, and harm the children's development - according to UNICEF, in Nepal, 85% of all children living in orphanages has at least one living parent. The rhetoric of such volunteer-sending organizations has also been argued to inform a "consumer-capitalist" culture that plays to the wants and needs of the privileged North, at the disadvantage of the Global South.

Ecotourism

Ecotourism is a form of tourism involving visiting fragile, pristine, and relatively undisturbed natural areas, intended as a low-impact and often small scale alternative to standard commercial mass tourism. It means responsible travel to natural areas, conserving the environment, and improving the well-being of the local people. Its purpose may be to educate the traveler, to provide funds for ecological conservation, to directly benefit the economic development and political empowerment of local communities, or to foster respect for different cultures and for human rights. Since the 1980s, ecotourism has been considered a critical endeavor by environmentalists, so that future generations may experience destinations relatively untouched by human intervention. Several university programs use this description as the working definition of ecotourism.

Llano del Muerto waterfall.

Generally, ecotourism deals with interaction with biotic components of the natural environments. Ecotourism focuses on socially responsible travel, personal growth, and environmental sustainability. Ecotourism typically involves travel to destinations where flora, fauna, and cultural heritage are the primary attractions. Ecotourism is intended to offer tourists an insight into the impact of human beings on the environment and to foster a greater appreciation of our natural habitats.

Responsible ecotourism programs include those that minimize the negative aspects of conventional tourism on the environment and enhance the cultural integrity of local people. Therefore, in addition to evaluating environmental and cultural factors, an integral part of ecotourism is the promotion of recycling, energy efficiency, water conservation, and creation of economic opportunities for local communities. For these reasons, ecotourism often appeals to advocates of environmental and social responsibility.

Many consider the term "ecotourism", like "sustainable tourism", an oxymoron. Like most forms of tourism, ecotourism generally depends on air transportation, which contributes to global climate change. Additionally, "the overall effect of sustainable tourism is negative where like ecotourism philanthropic aspirations mask hard-nosed immediate self-interest".

Criteria

Ecotourism is tourism which is conducted responsibly to conserve the environment and sustain the well-being of local people. It:

- Builds environmental awareness.

- Provides direct financial benefits for conservation.
- Provides financial benefits and empowerment for local people.
- Respects local culture.
- Supports human rights and democratic movements such as:
    - Conservation of biological diversity and cultural diversity through ecosystem protection.
    - Promotion of sustainable use of biodiversity, by providing jobs to local populations.
    - Sharing of all socio-economic benefits with local communities and indigenous peoples by having their informed consent and participation in the management of ecotourism enterprises.
    - Tourism to unspoiled natural resources, with minimal impact on the environment being a primary concern.
    - Minimization of tourism's own environmental impact.
    - Affordability and lack of waste in the form of luxury.
    - Local culture, flora, and fauna being the main attractions.
    - Local people, who benefit from this form of tourism economically, and often more than mass tourism.

The International Ecotourism Society defines ecotourism as "responsible travel to natural areas that conserves the environment, sustains the well-being of local people, and involves interpretation and education".

Seal watching near Malusi Islands.

For many countries, ecotourism is not simply a marginal activity to finance protection of the environment, but a major industry of the national economy. For example, in Costa Rica, Ecuador, Nepal, Kenya, Madagascar and territories such as Antarctica, ecotourism represents a significant portion of the gross domestic product and economic activity.

Ecotourism is often misinterpreted as any form of tourism that involves nature. Self-proclaimed practitioners and hosts of ecotourism experiences assume it is achieved by simply creating destinations in natural areas. According to critics of this commonplace and assumptive practice, true ecotourism must, above all, sensitize people to the beauty and the fragility of nature. These critics condemn some operators as greenwashing their operations: using the labels of "green" and "eco-friendly", while behaving in environmentally irresponsible ways.

Although academics disagree about who can be classified as an ecotourist and there is little statistical data, some estimate that more than five million ecotourists the majority of the ecotourist population come from the United States, with many others from Western Europe, Canada and Australia.

Currently, there are various moves to create national and international ecotourism accreditation programs, although the process is also controversial. National ecotourism certification programs have been put in place in countries such as Costa Rica, Australia, Kenya, Estonia, and Sweden.

Improving Sustainability

Principles

Ecotourism in both terrestrial and marine ecosystems can benefit conservation, provided the complexities of history, culture, and ecology in the affected regions are successfully navigated. Catherine Macdonald and colleagues identify the factors which determine conservation outcome, namely whether: animals and their habits are sufficiently protected; conflict between people and wildlife is avoided or at least suitably mitigated; there is good outreach and education of the local population into the benefits of ecotourism; there is effective collaboration with stakeholders in the area; and there is proper use of the money generated by ecotourism to conserve the local ecology. They conclude that ecotourism works best to conserve predators when the tourism industry is supported both politically and by the public, and when it is monitored and controlled at local, national, and international levels.

Small Scale, Slow Growth and Local Control

The underdevelopment theory of tourism describes a new form of imperialism by multinational corporations that control ecotourism resources. These corporations finance and profit from the development of large scale ecotourism that causes excessive environmental degradation, loss of traditional culture and way of life, and exploitation of local labor. In Zimbabwe and Nepal's Annapurna region, where underdevelopment is taking place, more than 90 percent of ecotourism revenues are expatriated to the parent countries, and less than 5 percent go into local communities.

The lack of sustainability highlights the need for small scale, slow growth, and locally based ecotourism. Local peoples have a vested interest in the well-being of their community, and are therefore more accountable to environmental protection than multinational corporations, though they receive very little of the profits. The lack of control, westernization, adverse impacts to the environment, loss of culture and traditions outweigh the benefits of establishing large scale ecotourism. Additionally, culture loss can be attributed to cultural commodification, in which local cultures are commodified in order to make a profit.

The increased contributions of communities to locally managed ecotourism create viable economic opportunities, including high-level management positions, and reduce environmental issues associated with poverty and unemployment. Because the ecotourism experience is marketed to a different lifestyle from large scale ecotourism, the development of facilities and infrastructure does not need to conform to corporate Western tourism standards, and can be much simpler and less expensive. There is a greater multiplier effect on the economy, because local products, materials, and labor are used. Profits accrue locally and import leakages are reduced. The Great Barrier Reef Park in Australia reported over half of a billion dollars of indirect income in the area and added thousands of indirect jobs between 2004 and 2005. However, even this form of tourism may require foreign investment for promotion or start up. When such investments are required, it is crucial for communities to find a company or non-governmental organization that reflects the philosophy of ecotourism; sensitive to their concerns and willing to cooperate at the expense of profit. The basic assumption of the multiplier effect is that the economy starts off with unused resources, for example, that many workers are cyclically unemployed and much of industrial capacity is sitting idle or incompletely utilized. By increasing demand in the economy, it is then possible to boost production. If the economy was already at full employment, with only structural, frictional, or other supply-side types of unemployment, any attempt to boost demand would only lead to inflation. For various laissez-faire schools of economics which embrace Say's Law and deny the possibility of Keynesian inefficiency and under-employment of resources, therefore, the multiplier concept is irrelevant or wrong-headed.

As an example, consider the government increasing its expenditure on roads by $1 million, without a corresponding increase in taxation. This sum would go to the road builders, who would hire more workers and distribute the money as wages and profits. The households receiving these incomes will save part of the money and spend the rest on consumer goods. These expenditures, in turn, will generate more jobs, wages, and profits, and so on with the income and spending circulating around the economy.

The multiplier effect arises because of the induced increases in consumer spending which occur due to the increased incomes and because of the feedback into increasing business revenues, jobs, and income again. This process does not lead to an economic explosion not only because of the supply-side barriers at potential output (full employment) but because at each "round", the increase in consumer spending is less than the increase in consumer incomes. That is, the marginal propensity to consume (MPC) is less than one, so that each round some extra income goes into saving, leaking out of the cumulative process. Each increase in spending is thus smaller than that of the previous round, preventing an explosion.

Efforts to Preserve Ecosystems at Risk

Some of the world's most exceptional biodiversity is located in the Galapagos Islands. These islands were designated a UNESCO World Heritage site in 1979, then added to UNESCO's List of World Heritage in Danger in 2007. IGTOA is a non-profit dedicated to preserving this unique living laboratory against the challenges of invasive species, human impact, and tourism. For travelers who want to be mindful of the environment and the impact of tourism, it is recommended to utilize an operator that is endorsed by a reputable ecotourism organization. In the case of the Galapagos, IGTOA has a list of the world's premiere Galapagos Islands tour companies dedicated to the lasting protection and preservation of the destination.

Natural Resource Management

Natural resource management can be utilized as a specialized tool for the development of ecotourism. There are several places throughout the world where a number of natural resources are abundant, but with human encroachment and habitats, these resources are depleting. Without the sustainable use of certain resources, they are destroyed, and floral and faunal species are becoming extinct. Ecotourism programs can be introduced for the conservation of these resources. Several plans and proper management programs can be introduced so that these resources remain untouched, and there are many organizations–including nonprofits and scientists working on this field.

In Southeast Asia government and nongovernmental organizations are working together with academics and industry operators to spread the economic benefits of tourism into the kampungs and villages of the region. A recently formed alliance, the South-East Asian Tourism Organisation (SEATO), is bringing together these diverse players to discuss resource management concerns.

A 2002, summit held in Quebec led to the 2008 Global Sustainable Tourism Criteria – a collaborative effort between the UN Foundation and other advocacy groups. The criteria, which are voluntary, involve the following standards: "effective sustainability planning, maximum social and economic benefits for local communities, minimum negative impacts on cultural heritage, and minimum negative impacts on the environment." There is no enforcing agency or system of punishments for summit.

Criticism

In the continuum of tourism activities that stretch from conventional tourism to ecotourism, there has been a lot of contention to the limit at which biodiversity preservation, local social-economic benefits, and environmental impact can be considered "ecotourism". For this reason, environmentalists, special interest groups, and governments define ecotourism differently. Environmental organizations have generally insisted that ecotourism is nature-based, sustainably managed, conservation supporting, and environmentally educated. The tourist industry and governments, however, focus more on the product aspect, treating ecotourism as equivalent to any sort of tourism based in nature. As a further complication, many terms are used under the rubric of ecotourism. Nature tourism, low impact tourism, green tourism, bio-tourism, ecologically responsible tourism, and others have been used in literature and marketing, although they are not necessarily synonymous with ecotourism.

The problems associated with defining ecotourism have often led to confusion among tourists and academics. Many problems are also subject of considerable public controversy and concern because of green washing, a trend towards the commercialization of tourism schemes disguised as sustainable, nature based, and environmentally friendly ecotourism. According to McLaren, these schemes are environmentally destructive, economically exploitative, and culturally insensitive at its worst. They are also morally disconcerting because they mislead tourists and manipulate their concerns for the environment. The development and success of such large scale, energy intensive, and ecologically unsustainable schemes are a testament to the tremendous profits associated with being labeled as ecotourism.

Negative Impact

Ecotourism has become one of the fastest-growing sectors of the tourism industry, growing annually by 10–15% worldwide. One definition of ecotourism is "the practice of low-impact, educational, ecologically and culturally sensitive travel that benefits local communities and host countries". Many of the ecotourism projects are not meeting these standards. Even if some of the guidelines are being executed, the local communities are still facing many of the negative impacts. South Africa is one of the countries that is reaping significant economic benefits from ecotourism, but the negative effects far outweigh the positive—including forcing people to leave their homes, gross violations of fundamental rights, and environmental hazards — far outweigh the medium-term economic benefits. A tremendous amount of money and human resources continue to be used for ecotourism despite unsuccessful outcomes, and even more, money is put into public relation campaigns to dilute the effects of criticism. Ecotourism channels resources away from other projects that could contribute more sustainable and realistic solutions to pressing social and environmental problems. "The money tourism can generate often ties parks and managements to ecotourism". But there is a tension in this relationship because ecotourism often causes conflict and changes in land-use rights, fails to deliver promises of community-level benefits, damages environments, and has many other social impacts. Indeed, many argue repeatedly that ecotourism is neither ecologically nor socially beneficial, yet it persists as a strategy for conservation and development due to the large profits. While several studies are being done on ways to improve the ecotourism structure, some argue that these examples provide a rationale for stopping it altogether. However, there are some positive examples, among them the Kavango-Zambezi Transfrontier Conservation Area (KAZA) and the Virunga National Park, as judged by WWF.

The ecotourism system exercises tremendous financial and political influence. The evidence above shows that a strong case exists for restraining such activities in certain locations. Funding could be used for field studies aimed at finding alternative solutions to tourism and the diverse problems Africa faces in result of urbanization, industrialization, and the overexploitation of agriculture. At the local level, ecotourism has become a source of conflict over control of land, resources, and tourism profits. In this case, ecotourism has harmed the environment and local people and has led to conflicts over profit distribution. In a perfect world, more efforts would be made towards educating tourists of the environmental and social effects of their travels. Very few regulations or laws stand in place as boundaries for the investors in ecotourism. These should be implemented to prohibit the promotion of unsustainable ecotourism projects and materials which project false images of destinations, demeaning local and indigenous culture.

Though conservation efforts in East Africa are indisputably serving the interests of tourism in the region it is important to make the distinction between conservation acts and the tourism industry. Eastern African communities are not the only of developing regions to experience economic and social harms from conservation efforts. Conservation in the Northwest Yunnan Region of China has similarly brought drastic changes to traditional land use in the region. Prior to logging restrictions imposed by the Chinese Government the industry made up 80 percent of the regions revenue. Following a complete ban on commercial logging the indigenous people of the Yunnan region now see little opportunity for economic development. Ecotourism may provide solutions to the economic hardships suffered from the loss of industry to conservation in the Yunnan in the same way that it may serve to remedy the difficulties faced by the Maasai. As stated, the ecotourism structure must be improved to direct more money into host communities by reducing leakages for the industry to be successful in alleviating poverty in developing regions, but it provides a promising opportunity.

Direct Environmental Impacts

Ecotourism operations occasionally fail to live up to conservation ideals. It is sometimes overlooked that ecotourism is a highly consumer-centered activity, and that environmental conservation is a means to further economic growth.

Although ecotourism is intended for small groups, even a modest increase in population, however temporary, puts extra pressure on the local environment and necessitates the development of additional infrastructure and amenities. The construction of water treatment plants, sanitation facilities, and lodges come with the exploitation of non-renewable energy sources and the utilization of already limited local resources. The conversion of natural land to such tourist infrastructure is implicated in deforestation and habitat deterioration of butterflies in Mexico and squirrel monkeys in Costa Rica. In other cases, the environment suffers because local communities are unable to meet the infrastructure demands of ecotourism. The lack of adequate sanitation facilities in many East African parks results in the disposal of campsite sewage in rivers, contaminating the wildlife, livestock, and people who draw drinking water from it.

Aside from environmental degradation with tourist infrastructure, population pressures from ecotourism also leaves behind garbage and pollution associated with the Western lifestyle. Although ecotourists claim to be educationally sophisticated and environmentally concerned, they rarely understand the ecological consequences of their visits and how their day-to-day activities append physical impacts on the environment. As one scientist observes, they "rarely acknowledge how the meals they eat, the toilets they flush, the water they drink, and so on, are all part of broader regional economic and ecological systems they are helping to reconfigure with their very activities." Nor do ecotourists recognize the great consumption of non-renewable energy required to arrive at their destination, which is typically more remote than conventional tourism destinations. For instance, an exotic journey to a place 10,000 kilometers away consumes about 700 liters of fuel per person.

Ecotourism activities are, in and of themselves, issues in environmental impact because they may disturb fauna and flora. Ecotourists believe that because they are only taking pictures and leaving footprints, they keep ecotourism sites pristine, but even harmless-sounding activities such as nature hikes can be ecologically destructive. In the Annapurna Circuit in Nepal, ecotourists have worn down the marked trails and created alternate routes, contributing to soil impaction, erosion, and plant damage. Where the ecotourism activity involves wildlife viewing, it can scare away animals, disrupt their feeding and nesting sites, or acclimate them to the presence of people. In Kenya, wildlife-observer disruption drives cheetahs off their reserves, increasing the risk of inbreeding and further endangering the species.

Environmental Hazards

The industrialization, urbanization and agricultural practices of human society are having a serious impact on the environment. Ecotourism is now also considered to be playing a role in environmental depletion including deforestation, disruption of ecological life systems and various forms of pollution, all of which contribute to environmental degradation. For example, the number of motor vehicles crossing a park increases as tour drivers search for rare species. The number of roads disrupts the grass cover, which has serious consequences on plant and animal species. These areas also have a higher rate of disturbances and invasive species due to increasing traffic off of the beaten path into new, undiscovered areas. Ecotourism also has an effect on species through the value placed on them. “Certain species have gone from being little known or valued by local people to being highly valued commodities. The commodification of plants may erase their social value and lead to overproduction within protected areas. Local people and their images can also be turned into commodities”. Kamuaro points out the relatively obvious contradiction that any commercial venture into unspoiled, pristine land inevitably means a higher pressure on the environment.

Local People

Most forms of ecotourism are owned by foreign investors and corporations that provide few benefits to the local people. An overwhelming majority of profits are put into the pockets of investors instead of reinvestment into the local economy or environmental protection leading to further environmental degradation. The limited numbers of local people who are employed in the economy enter at its lowest level and are unable to live in tourist areas because of meager wages and a two-market system.

In some cases, the resentment by local people results in environmental degradation. As a highly publicized case, the Maasai nomads in Kenya killed wildlife in national parks but are now helping the national park to save the wildlife to show aversion to unfair compensation terms and displacement from traditional lands. The lack of economic opportunities for local people also constrains them to degrade the environment as a means of sustenance. The presence of affluent ecotourists encourage the development of destructive markets in wildlife souvenirs, such as the sale of coral trinkets on tropical islands and animal products in Asia, contributing to illegal harvesting and poaching from the environment. In Suriname, sea turtle reserves use a very large portion of their budget to guard against these destructive activities.

Displacement of People

One of the worst examples of communities being moved in order to create a park is the story of the Maasai. About 70% of national parks and game reserves in East Africa are on Maasai land. The first negative impact of tourism was the land lost from the Maasai culture. Local and national governments took advantage of the Maasai’s ignorance on the situation and robbed them of huge chunks of grazing land, putting to risk their only socio-economic livelihood. In Kenya, the Maasai also have not gained any economic benefits. Despite the loss of their land, employment favors better-educated workers. Furthermore, the investors in this area are not local and have not put any profits back into the local economy. In some cases, game reserves can be created without informing or consulting the local people. They only find out when an eviction notice is delivered. Another source of resentment is the manipulation of the local people by their government. “Eco-tourism works to create simplistic images of local people and their uses and understandings of their surroundings. Through the lens of these simplified images, officials direct policies and projects towards the local people and the local people are blamed if the projects fail” (West, 2006). Clearly, tourism as a trade is not empowering the local people who make it rich and satisfying. Instead, ecotourism exploits and depletes, particularly in African Maasai tribes. It has to be reoriented if it is to be useful to local communities and to become sustainable.

Threats to Indigenous Cultures

Ecotourism often claims that it preserves and "enhances" local cultures. Evidence shows that with the establishment of protected areas local people have illegally lost their homes, and mostly with no compensation. Pushing people onto marginal lands with harsh climates, poor soils, lack of water, and infested with livestock and disease does little to enhance livelihoods even when a proportion of ecotourism profits are directed back into the community. The establishment of parks can create harsh survival realities and deprive the people of their traditional use of land and natural resources. Ethnic groups are increasingly being seen as a "backdrop" to the scenery and wildlife. The local people struggle for cultural survival and freedom of cultural expression while being "observed" by tourists. Local indigenous people also have a strong resentment towards the change, "Tourism has been allowed to develop with virtually no controls. Too many lodges have been built, too much firewood is being used and no limits are being placed on tourism vehicles. They regularly drive off-track and harass the wildlife. Their vehicle tracks criss-cross the entire Masai Mara. Inevitably the bush is becoming eroded and degraded."

Mismanagement

While governments are typically entrusted with the administration and enforcement of environmental protection, they often lack the commitment or capability to manage ecotourism sites. The regulations for environmental protection may be vaguely defined, costly to implement, hard to enforce, and uncertain in effectiveness. Government regulatory agencies, are susceptible to making decisions that spend on politically beneficial but environmentally unproductive projects. Because of prestige and conspicuousness, the construction of an attractive visitor's center at an ecotourism site may take precedence over more pressing environmental concerns like acquiring habitat, protecting endemic species, and removing invasive ones. Finally, influential groups can pressure, and sway the interests of the government to their favor. The government and its regulators can become vested in the benefits of the ecotourism industry which they are supposed to regulate, causing restrictive environmental regulations and enforcement to become more lenient.

Management of ecotourism sites by private ecotourism companies offers an alternative to the cost of regulation and deficiency of government agencies. It is believed that these companies have a self-interest in limited environmental degradation because tourists will pay more for pristine environments, which translates to higher profit. However, theory indicates that this practice is not economically feasible and will fail to manage the environment.

The model of monopolistic competition states that distinctiveness will entail profits, but profits will promote imitation. A company that protects its ecotourism sites is able to charge a premium for the novel experience and pristine environment. But when other companies view the success of this approach, they also enter the market with similar practices, increasing competition and reducing demand. Eventually, the demand will be reduced until the economic profit is zero. A cost-benefit analysis shows that the company bears the cost of environmental protection without receiving the gains. Without economic incentive, the whole premise of self-interest through environmental protection is quashed; instead, ecotourism companies will minimize environment related expenses and maximize tourism demand.

The tragedy of the commons offers another model for economic unsustainability from environmental protection, in ecotourism sites utilized by many companies. Although there is a communal incentive to protect the environment, maximizing the benefits in the long run, a company will conclude that it is in their best interest to utilize the ecotourism site beyond its sustainable level. By increasing the number of ecotourists, for instance, a company gains all the economic benefit while paying only a part of the environmental cost. In the same way, a company recognizes that there is no incentive to actively protect the environment; they bear all the costs, while the benefits are shared by all other companies. The result, again, is mismanagement.

Taken together, the mobility of foreign investment and lack of economic incentive for environmental protection means that ecotourism companies are disposed to establishing themselves in new sites once their existing one is sufficiently degraded.

In addition, the systematic literature review conducted by Cabral and Dhar have identified several challenges due to slow progression of ecotourism initiatives such as (a) economic leakages, (b) lack of government involvement, (c) skill deficiency among the local communities, (d) absence of disseminating environmental education, (e) sporadic increase in pollution, (f) conflict between tourism management personnel and local communities and (g) inadequate infrastructure development.

Niche Tourism

A 'niche' tourism strategy is one that appeals to a small number of people who are especially interested in something. Another way to describe 'niche' tourism is 'specialised' tourism.

Examples of niche tourism are:

- Adventure tourism: Climbing major mountain peaks is difficult, and requires lots of training, planning and equipment. Most tourists could not do this type of tourism. Examples include the Nepalese Himalayan mountains with Mount Everest the top attraction.

- Movie location tourism: While many people would be happy to visit a place used as a location for a movie set, few people make it the main focus of their holiday. Examples of places that have a specialised focus are Salzberg (the location of the Sound of Music), and New Zealand (location for the Lord of the Rings trilogy). The principle also extends to TV-set tourism such as Game of Thrones sets in Spain, Northern Ireland and Croatia.
- Heritage tourism: Mostly focused on history and culture, this type of tourism is increasingly popular but remains relatively small-scale compared to the mass tourism of beach holidays. Examples of locations that market themselves for heritage tourism include many Italian cities (such as Venice, an example of a tourism hotspot), the Beijing (the Forbidden Palace and the Great Wall), and Machu Picchu in Peru.

There are many other examples of niche tourism including (but not limited to):

- Nature tourism: Going on safari or to see a particular landscape such as Victoria Falls on the Zambezi river.
- Remote tourism: Visiting locations that few people can go to because of the difficulty of getting there (and the lack of facilities at the destination), such as the Amazon rainforest or Antarctica.
- Photography tourism: Small companies offer photography.
- Homestay tourism: Tourists reside with a family in their regular home for their visit, and join the family in their regular activities such as farming.
- Volunteer tourism: Tourists join in education, conservation and other charitable projects.

Niche Tourism: Benefits and Risks

Niche tourism is often promoted by national tourism strategies because it is seen as a more sustainable way of developing tourism:

- There are relatively low numbers of tourists.
- They are genuinely interested in seeing the destination as it is, rather than demanding changes to it such as more hotel facilities.
- They are often willing to pay more to see a unique environment.

Therefore, the tourist attraction (such as architecture, local culture, a rainforest and so on) is more likely to be preserved because it is now economically and socially valuable to the country. This means conservation efforts are more successful and the tourism is more sustainable.

However, niche tourism must be carefully chosen. This is because of several negative factors:

- There are relatively few tourists, so it is unlikely to be scaled up as a huge growth industry.
- Niche tourism is susceptible to 'shock' events. For example, if terrorism begins to affect

people visiting religious buildings, those tourists might not travel – which means the whole tourist industry is at risk.

- Niche tourism often attracts people from a very specific demographic, whose tastes may change too quickly for the destination to adapt. For example, a TV set location may be popular only as long as the TV show is on the air, after which tourism may decline.
- Because of the relatively small number of tourists, a destination may suddenly lose its customers because of competition. For example, an island might have a tourists but then an island in the new location improves its tourist infrastructure and people choose to go elsewhere.
- Too many niche tourists means too many people doing the same thing, resulting in those same tourists having a negative experience. A good example is scuba diving off some Thai islands, where the number of visitors has put off some from going back.
- Family decisions about holidays usually involve compromise. If the destination caters to only one type of tourist, that person may not go to the destination because there is nothing for their partner or family to do.
- Promotion of a single niche can put other people off going to the location. Potential tourists may not realise that there are other things to do and decide to go somewhere else.

Global Sphere of Influence

Many niche tourist destinations have relatively low levels of participation in per capita terms – i.e. there aren't enough people living within the country to make the tourist activity worthwhile for companies to offer it. Therefore they must appeal to a global audience to ensure there are enough visitors to be a viable tourist destination. This is known as a global sphere of influence.

City Tourism

City tourism or also called urban tourism is a type of tourism where is located in the large human agglomerations, usually in the main cities of each country.

Row of tourist buses in front of the Berlin Cathedral and the Altes Museum.

According to the World Tourism Organization (UNWTO), urban tourism is defined as "a type of tourism activity which takes place in an urban space with its inherent attributes characterized by non-agricultural based economy such as administration, manufacturing, trade and services and by being nodal points of transport. Urban/city destinations offer a broad and heterogeneous range of cultural, architectural, technological, social and natural experiences and products for leisure and business."

Activities

A guided tour around the 9/11 Tribute Museum in Manhattan.

There are different activities carried out by city tourists, among them the visit to buildings within a city, such as museums and art galleries, religious temples, skyscrapers and buildings with some historical interest, monuments and memorials, cemeteries, etc. There is also another modality of city tourism associated with attendance at massive events, such as festivals, concerts, parades, conferences, demonstrations and protests, etc. Tourist activities linked to nightlife and cultural tourism are also typical of city tourism, due to the supply that exists in the most populated areas. In the same way, there is a correlation between city tourism and shopping tourism, especially for people from smaller towns or countryside, who take advantage of sightseeing while shopping.

City Tours

Tour operators have a varied offer of tourism packages that include visits within a specific city, as well as several cities within a country or continent. In addition, expert tourist guides are available in cities with a large influx of tourists.

Enotourism

Enotourism, oenotourism, wine tourism, or vinitourism refers to tourism whose purpose is or includes the tasting, consumption or purchase of wine, often at or near the source. Where other types of tourism are often passive in nature, enotourism can consist of visits to wineries, tasting wines, vineyard walks, or even taking an active part in the harvest.

Wine museum at Graffigna, San Juan.

Enotourism is a relatively new form of tourism. Its history varies greatly from region to region, but in places such as the Napa Valley AVA and Wine Country, it saw heavy growth once a concerted marketing effort was implemented in 1975 that was given a further boost by the 1976 Judgment of Paris.

Typical winery tasting room.

Other regions, such as Catalonia, Spain have only started marketing enotourism starting in the mid-2000s, primarily focusing on how it is an alternative form of tourism to the beach for which Spain is overall known.

There was also a rise in the profile of enotourism among English speakers with the 2004 release of the film, Sideways whose two central characters visit wineries and wine in the Santa Barbara region of Southern California.

The industry around enotourism has grown significantly throughout the first decade of the 21st century. In the United States 27 million travelers, or 17% of American leisure travelers, engaged in culinary or wine-related activities. In Italy the figure stands at approximately five million travelers, generating 2.5 billion euros in revenue.

"Enotourism Day" is celebrated on the second Sunday of November each year to promote cellar visits in Germany, Austria, Slovenia, Spain, France, Greece, Hungary, Italy, and Portugal. In North America, the first Wine Tourism Day was established for May 11, 2013 with events scheduled throughout the continent.

Chile has grown its enotourism industry in recent years, with several tourist routes being opened throughout the country, with several of them offering overnight accommodations.

Activities

Cycling through vineyards in Mendoza.

Most visits to the wineries take place at or near the site where the wine is produced. Visitors typically learn the history of the winery, see how the wine is made, and then taste the wines. At some wineries, staying in a small guest house at the winery is also offered. Many visitors buy the wines made by the winery at the premises, accounting for up to 33% of their annual sales.

Very small, low production regions such as Priorat, Catalonia focus on small, intimate visits with the owner as the host and include walks through the vineyards to help visitors understand the unique qualities of the region.

More elaborate tastings can include horizontal and vertical tastings as well as full meals focused upon showcasing the wines.

As the enotourism industry matures, additional activities have been added to visits such as riding electrically assisted bicycles, called, "burricleta".

Business Tourism

Business tourism or business travel is a more limited and focused subset of regular tourism. During business tourism (traveling), individuals are still working and being paid, but are doing so away from both their workplace and home.

Some definitions of tourism exclude business travel. However, the World Tourism Organization (UNWTO) defines tourists as people "traveling to and staying in places outside their usual environment for not more than one consecutive year for leisure, business and other purposes".

Primary business tourism activities include meetings, and attending conferences and exhibitions. Despite the term business in business tourism, when individuals from government or non-profit organizations engage in similar activities, this is still categorized as business tourism (travel).

Historically, business tourism takes the form of traveling to, spending money and staying abroad, being away for some time, and has a history as long as that of international trade. In late 20th century, business tourism was seen as a major industry.

According to the 1998 data from the British Tourist Authority and National Tourist Boards, business tourism accounted for about 14% of all trips to or within the UK, and 15% of the tourist market within the UK. A 2005 estimate suggested that those numbers for UK may be closer to 30%. Sharma (2004) cited a UNWTO estimated that business tourism accounts for 30% of international tourism, through its importance varies significantly between different countries.

Characteristics

Compared to regular tourism, business tourism involves a smaller section of the population, with different motivations, and additional freedom-of-choice-limiting constraints imposed through the business aspects. Destinations of business tourism are much more likely to be areas significantly developed for business purposes (cities, industrial regions, etc.). An average business tourist is more wealthy than an average leisure tourist, and is expected to spend more money.

Business tourism can be divided into primary and secondary activities. Primary ones are -business (work)-related, and included activities such as consultancy, inspections, and attending meetings. Secondary ones are related to tourism (leisure) and include activities such as dining out, recreation, shopping, sightseeing, meeting others for leisure activities, and so on. While the primary ones tend to be seen as more important, the secondary ones are nonetheless often described as "substantial".

Business tourism can involve individual and small-group travel, and destinations can include small to larger meetings, including conventions and conferences, trade fairs, and exhibitions. In the US, about half of business tourism involves attending a large meeting of some kind.

Most tourist facilities, such as airports, restaurants and hotels, are shared between leisure and business tourists, through a seasonal difference is often apparent (for example, business tourism may use those facilities during times less attractive for leisure tourists, such as when the weather conditions are less attractive).

Business tourism can be divided into:

- Traditional business traveling, or meetings: Intended for face-to-face meetings with business partners in different locations.
- Incentive trips: A job perk, aimed at motivating employees (for example, approximately a third of UK companies use this strategy to motivate workers).
- Conference and exhibition traveling: Intended for attending large-scale meetings. In an estimated number of 14,000 conferences worldwide (for 1994), primary destinations are Paris, London, Madrid, Geneva, Brussels, Washington, New York, Sydney and Singapore.

The words meetings, incentive, conferences and exhibition in the context of business tourism are abbreviated as MICE.

Sports Tourism

Sports tourism refers to travel which involves either observing or participating in a sporting event while staying apart from the tourists' usual environment. Sport tourism is a fast-growing sector of the global travel industry.

Classification of Sport Tourism

There are several classifications of sport tourism. Gammon and Robinson suggested that sports tourism can be categorized as *Hard Sports Tourism* or *Soft Sports Tourism*, while Gibson suggested that there are three types of sports tourism: *Sports Event Tourism, Celebrity and Nostalgia Sport Tourism* and *Active Sport Tourism.*

Hard and Soft Sport Tourism

The "hard" definition of sport tourism refers to the quantity of people participating at a competitive sport events. Normally these kinds of events are the motivation that attract visitors to the events. Olympic Games, FIFA World Cup, F1 Grand Prix and regional events such as NASCAR Sprint Cup Series could be described as hard sports tourism.

The "soft" definition of sport tourism is when the tourist travels to participate in recreational sporting, or signing up for leisure interests. Hiking, skiing, running and canoeing can be described as soft sports tourism. Perhaps the most common form of soft sports tourism involves golf in regards to destinations in Europe and the United States. A large number of people are interested in playing some of the world's greatest and highest ranked courses, and take great pride in checking those destinations off of their list of places to visit.

Sports Event Tourism

Sports event tourism refers to the visitors who visit a city to watch events. The two events that attract the most tourists worldwide are the Olympics and the FIFA World Cup. These events held once every four years, in a different city in the world. Sport tourism in the United States is more focused on events that happen annually. The major event for the National Football League is the Super Bowl, held at the end of the year in different city every year. Even though the National Hockey League started the annual NHL Winter Classic game in 2008, the 2014 New Year's outdoor hockey game rivaled the Stanley Cup Tournament in popularity and "revitalized the NHL". As of 2015, the newest trend in college basketball was to start the season off with annual tournaments such as the Maui Invitational held in Hawaii, and the Battle for Atlantis which is played in the Bahamas. This idea of pairing quality sports events with the Bahamas attractions raised the island's profile and brought in more visitors and dollars to the country. The Battle for Atlantis brought more than 5,000 fans in during Thanksgiving week for the three-day tournament. The event helped increase hotel capacity from what is typically around 60 percent this time of year to 90 percent. Sport tourism "is a growing market and many different cities and countries want to be involved".

Celebrity and Nostalgia Sport Tourism

Celebrity and nostalgia sport tourism involves visits to the sports halls of fame and venue and meeting sports personalities in a vacation basis.

Active Sport Tourism

Active sport tourism refers to those who participate in the sports or sport events. Rugby football,

football, basketball, etc are considered active sports and many sport events (which we call tournaments or festivals) are organized each year in most of the countries in the world.

Culinary Tourism

Culinary tourism or food tourism is the exploration of food as the purpose of tourism. It is now considered a vital component of the tourism experience. Dining out is common among tourists and "food is believed to rank alongside climate, accommodation, and scenery" in importance to tourists.

Culinary tourism.

Culinary or food tourism is the pursuit of unique and memorable eating and drinking experiences, both near and far. Culinary tourism differs from agritourism in that culinary tourism is considered a subset of cultural tourism (cuisine is a manifestation of culture) whereas agritourism is considered a subset of rural tourism, but culinary tourism and agritourism are inextricably linked, as the seeds of cuisine can be found in agriculture. Culinary/food tourism is not limited to gourmet food. Food tourism can be considered a subcategory of experiential travel.

While many cities, regions or countries are known for their food, culinary tourism is not limited by food culture. Every tourist eats about three times a day, making food one of the fundamental economic drivers of tourism. Countries like Ireland, Peru and Canada are making significant investment in culinary tourism development and are seeing results with visitor spending and overnight stays rising as a result of food tourism promotion and product development.

The World Food Travel Association offers the following clarification and definition:

We say "food tourism", but drinking beverages is an implied and associated activity. It is also cumbersome to say "food and drink tourism". We need to clarify "far and near". In addition to traveling across country or the world to eat or drink, we can also be food travelers in our own regions, cities and neighborhoods. If you rarely leave your neighborhood and travel across town to a new neighborhood to go to a special grocery store or to eat out, you're a "food traveler" in your own backyard! The act of traveling is implied because most people travel at least across their own town, if not the region, the country and even the planet. The distance covered is not as important as the fact that we are always on the move. We are all "travelers" of a sort and we are all "eaters". Therefore, we can also all be regarded as "food travelers". Previously the World Food Travel Association had used the phrase "culinary tourism" to describe our industry. We stopped using that phrase in 2012 because our research indicated that it gave a misleading impression. While "culinary" technically can be used for anything relating to food and drink and initially seems to make good sense, the perception among the majority of English-speakers we interviewed is that the word "culinary" is elitist. Nothing could be further from the truth about what our industry is all about. "Food Tourism" includes [sic] the food carts and street vendors as much as the locals-only (gastro)pubs, dramatic wineries, or one-of-a-kind restaurants. There is something for everyone in the food tourism industry.

Food tourism has four general types:

- Cooking class.
- Food tours.
- Wine, beer and food festivals.
- Specialty dining experiences.

Economic Impact

Culinary tourism became prominent in 2001. The World Food Travel Association estimates that food and beverage expenses account for 15% to 35% of all tourism spending, depending on the affordability of the destination. The WFTA lists possible food tourism benefits as including more visitors, more sales, more media attention, increased tax revenue, and greater community pride.

Cooking Classes

A growing area of culinary tourism is cooking classes. The formats vary from a short lesson lasting a few hours to full-day and multi-day courses. The focus for foreign tourists will usually be on the cuisine of the country they are visiting, whereas local tourists may be keen to experience cuisines new to them. Many cooking classes also include market tours to enhance the cultural experience.

Food Tours

Pasztecik szczeciński is one of traditional dishes of Pomerania.

The food tour formula varies from tour to tour and from operator to operator (of which there are many). Most, however, feature the following elements:

- They operate in major cities, generally but not always capital cities, that have substantial tourist numbers. Tours exist – amongst other places - in London, Paris, Rome, Florence, Toronto, Istanbul, New York City, Lisbon, Berlin, Madrid, Belfast, San Francisco, Copenhagen, Tokyo, Shanghai, Beijing, Athens, Kuala Lumpur, Marrakech and Barcelona. Operators must find a city with a vibrant and interesting food culture. Street food may feature.
- Tours are generally on foot. The distances traveled are never large – sometimes as in the Indian Food Tour of London, they are focused on a few adjoining streets. Few tourists seem to want a cycle tour although one or two cycle tour companies are considering a food element.
- Tours typically last for a minimum of three hours, although many last longer. Many tours start around 11:00 am local time and continue well into the afternoon, making it the day's major attraction. Additionally, more and more tour companies are adding evening tour options. Tours generally start and end at public transport hubs such as metro stations.
- Participant numbers vary, but 12 to 16 is generally considered the upper limit.
- Tours rarely charge for small children who share food with parents/carers. Tours may not be necessarily fully compliant with wheelchair use – this will depend on the exact tour and the attitude of each location to disability.
- Tours take visitors to places they might otherwise not have seen, so they can shop and eat like locals rather than rely on tourist "traps". Phrases such as "eat the city like a real Parisian/Berliner/Londoner/New Yorker" are often employed in food tour publicity.
- All tours are guided by local people. Many tour guides add their local knowledge as a bonus, perhaps recommending restaurants in other parts of the city.
- Tours are primarily about food. The format varies from company to company but will generally include visits to markets, bars, and cafés where those on the tour are invited to

sample the wares. There is usually a shop visit to buy the sort of food that is difficult to source elsewhere. Tours may end up with a sit-down meal at a restaurant where there is usually the choice of beer, wine or soft drinks.

- Guides talk about food, often pointing those on the tour to shops they use. They may discuss how the sort of food they and their families eat differs from the food generally offered to tourists. They are unlikely to be kindly disposed to international fast food outlets.
- Guides generally add material about the history of the area the tour is in. Most tours are close to, but not in, major tourist zones.
- Tours assume that participants eat almost anything and are not designed for special diets. However, most can accommodate vegetarians although vegan diets are rarely catered for. The same warning applies to those looking for gluten-free or other restrictive diets.
- Many tour companies aim to create a sustainable tourism model over which they provide to their clients an experience that makes a positive impact on the local environment, society and economy by working only with local producers and/or family own establishments, and celebrating local traditions, all on foot, which means having a zero carbon footprint.

Extreme Tourism

Extreme tourism brings together the most specialized form of tourist activities. In contented societies, living in concrete and asphalt landscape, people began to look for the possibility of letting off steam in nature and rebound stress. they adore risks and madness. Walkers attempt to overcome the one-off 100 km and more, kayakers floating down from the mountains rushing rivers, the riders are pushing the peaks of mountain paths, skiers come to ski on high peaks on snowmobile untouched snow cover.

Causes of Extreme Tourism Interest

Increasingly popular among young people becomes sports at increased risk, called extreme sports.

These are sports whose practice requires extraordinary skill and courage to bear high risk, and also very often a threat to life. Sports with an increased risk, are all involving outside routes or areas not prepared for regular sport activity. Extreme sports include, in particular: base jumping, caving, air sports, mountain biking, motocross, riding on jet skis, motorboat racing, or high mountain climbing.

Rafting on rushing mountain river, jump rope, or other extreme sports require a lot of courage. However, there are people who can not live without extreme experiences, and practicing such sports gives meaning to their lives. It may be due to the fact that when someone tries once, it is difficult to stop because of excitement and elevated adrenaline level.

Extreme Water Tourism Activities

- Canyoning: Is a field invented by tourists practicing mountaineering, canoeing, climbing and cave exploration. It involves long hours of arduous climbing with sophisticated hardware for runoff narrow, steep gorges of mountain rivers.

To the pond located at the foot of the hill. Along the way they must steer clear of stones and boulders sticking out towards them.

- Hydrospeeding: Based on overcoming mountain rivers with the flow on a small plastic board, in an appropriate protective attire (neoprene suit, helmet, flippers, protectors on the knees and elbows).
- Canoe Slalom: Grown on rushing mountain rivers.
- Freediving: Breath-hold diving.
- Diving: Free diving and snorkeling includes scuba diving underwater on apnea from 50m to 100-800m, spearfishing, underwater navigation on the route, as well as underwater team games.

Underwater tourism are performed in the following forms:

- Diving breath-hold:
  - Deep diving,
  - Spearfishing.
- Free swimming using diving duit:
  - Wreck exploration,
  - Cave diving,
  - Under ice diving,
  - Night diving.
- Kiteboarding: Which is the kind of gliding on the surfboard after jumping from airplane.

- Often with aerobatics, and parachute landing.
- Wakeboarding: Involving gliding and surfing after motorboat.
- Windsurfing: Gliding on special board with a sail.

Extreme Tourism on Land

- Adventure racing: Usually a form of long-distance run on orientation (from several to several hundred kilometers), combining trekking, mountain biking, swimming and ski running.
- Climbing: The movement of the ground so steep that it requires use of hands to maintain balance. There are many types of climbing, including climbing on rocks several meters high (bouldering) and climbing to more than eight thousand peaks in Himalayas. It is performed using natural features of rock and terrain. Climbing equipment is only used for belaying in the event of a fall. There is also solo climb, which does not use any belaying or protective equipment.
- Aving: Involves the examination and exploration of caves and spelunking. Most are performed in hard to access and dangerous places. In many caves are present narrow straits, traps, cliffs, places, threatening to collapse and falls off the rocks.
- Base jumping: Which is kind of parachuting from buildings, antenna masts, bridges and rocks, the acronym "BASE" is derived from: Building, Antenna, Span, Earth.
- Bungejumping: Jumping from high places on the rubber tied to the legs, for example bridges, brackets, structures, rock cliffs.
- Jumping dream: The essence of which is the zip on line between two tall buildings, rocks, or over the ravine.
- Mountain biking: On marked trails and bike paths, forest roads and off-road, for example: downhill.
- Motocross: A form of motorcycle racing performed on special tracks. Motocross tracks are usually intentionally piled up with sand, clay or mud.
- Parkour: Involves overcoming urban obstacles in an effective way.
- Mountainboarding: Which involves riding down the steep slope, on a board with wheels.
- Paintball: An outdoor war game, using specially designed air gun, sling bullets with paint.
- Streetluge: Which is a fast descent on a trolley with wheels on the steep and winding asphalt roads.
- Ski alpinism: Which combines mountain downhill skiing, climbing and hiking mountain in winter and skiing, requires great physical, fitness, knowledge of the specificities of mountains, climbing skills and sophisticated equipment.

Extreme Air Tourism

- Paragliding: Sport and a form of recreation which consists of flying with a paraglider. Is one of the most popular aviation sports.
- Skydiving with parachute: Sport involving the performance of jumps, in which depending on the discipline is assessed component of stroke, e.g. to perform acrobatics in free fall, performing acrobatics in the open canopy or precision landing.
- Skysurfing: Skydiving on a snowboard.
- Hang gliding: Is a form of flying with the glider, which wing is stretched on the aluminum or plastic rack. By using internal combustion engine hang gliding becomes motor gliding.

Mass Tourism

Mass tourism is the act of visiting a leisure destination with large amounts of people at one time. The development of mass tourism is parallel to the development and improvements of technology. Transportation and internet has evolved so much in time, making communication fast and easy, this allows tourist to research, find out and book and even pay for their holidays online, this thus contributing to the rise of mass tourism, besides that the improvement in technology in the transportation industry also helps in the transport of large numbers of people in a short space of time to places of leisure interest, so that greater numbers of people could begin to enjoy the benefits of leisure time.

Mass tourism has always been the subject of criticism for its negative impacts around the world. Mass tourism's potentially destructive impacts on societies, culture and environment. Many authors condemned and still condemn this mass consumption and those who enjoy it. Actually the debate over the advantages and the disadvantages of tourism has raged incessantly and will continue. Tourism development in many places, and especially mass tourism, has led to deterioration in environment quality. In the 1960s, the effects of mass tourism and the increasing awareness of the human impacts on the environment led to a general state that nature is not an inexhaustible resource.

Relation between Environment and Tourism

Today, people are being more sensibility for the natural environment, this is because the tourism industry is the only economical sector that uses a destinations natural environment as a very important part of its product. In other words, the natural environment is a key element of the tourism activity. Krippendorf "the landscape is the real raw material of tourism; it is the reason for the existence of tourism as well as its economic driving force". This highlights that tourism product quality is linked with environment quality, and it's highly dependence between tourism and environment because its often used as basic argument to make the tourism industry aware about the negative impacts of mass tourism on the environment.

Environment

The environment can be considered as a tourism resource and is a part of the tourism product because tourism is directly affected by environmental quality. This close relationship or interdependence between tourism and environment, can be defines it as "the environmental part of tourism".

Multiple surveys confirm the hypothesis that the quality of natural environment constitutes "the primary factors that attracted the present-day tourist". So, if tourism wants to survive, it seems imperative to reach this harmony between people and nature. It is the only way to minimize the costs of tourism on the environment and permit the tourist to enjoy undisturbed nature. This "symbiotic relation", term used by Budowski has a name, it is sustainable tourism.

Mass tourism creates intense environmental pressures due to the fact that such activity involves a large number of tourists in small areas. Moreover, those pressures are accentuated by the temporal polarization of mass tourism. Hudman and Jackson acknowledge that coastal resorts are a good example of changing pre-existing forms associated with both the human and physical environment. In Spain, for example, several coastal villages have been changed rather dramatically in the past few years. Travel posters of the area usually highlight the area as it was before tourism. Yet, with the growth of mass tourism, the scattered villages of Torremolinos, Benidorm or Lloret del Mar, and other small villages are no longer recognizable. Lloret de Mar, was among the first in Europe to be developed for mass tourism. More recently, the development of transport facilities such as airlines have permitted to those places to attract still more tourists. For example, since the arrival of Ryanair, the low cost airline company, at Gerona airport, the town of Lloret de Mar has become far more accessible, especially to those who maintain a strict travel budget. Mass tourism has a range of impacts of all types on natural environment (e.g. coastal, mountains or inland) but also on built environments (e.g. historic sites or cities).

Mass tourism leads to the direct degradation, pollution, even destruction of elements (air, soils, geology, vegetation, water and wildlife) and ecosystems (coastal, mountains, inland and polar). The main causes are the construction of tourist facilities such as hotel complexes, theme parks and marinas and the concentration of tourists in the same place. The simplest way to view such environmental impacts is to consider mass tourism within specific environments. Coastal areas are especially vulnerable to mass tourism because they represent the most desirable places to spend vacation. In some places such as the Mediterranean, there has been widespread destruction of the ecosystems. It is the marine ecosystem which supports and is affected by mass beach tourism, especially concentrated during the high season (from June to August). The summer months have most sun and they include the longest school holiday period when families take their main vacation. The marine ecosystems suffer from garbage disposal by hotels and littering by tourists, oil spills from cruise ships and other motorized boat traffic, etc. All the construction of tourism facilities required for mass tourism in coastal areas affects the beach in any ways. Infrastructures are required to cope with the large volume of consumers in a short period of time.

Why did Mass Tourism Happen?

Mass tourism appears after the World War II, it was initiated in the back streets of the industrial towns and cities in the north of England. The development of mass tourism in the western world was linked to the economic development of society and as a matter of fact to the incorporation of a more powerful middle and lower class inside the tourist market. This expansion has been based on external factors such as generalisation of paid holidays, rising standards of living and a rapid improvement in the means of transportation such as the increase in air travel. The growth of such tourism represents a democratisation of travel and this democratisation means that status distinctions will be drawn between the different classes of traveller, but less between those that can travel or not. There are a lot of factors which have or can cause an increase in tourism which then results in the mass tourism phenomenon, the development of the demographic in Malaysia plays an important role in contributing to the increase in tourism activity. First would be the increase in wealth, Malaysia's middle class has increased tremendously through the years, and this is because of the modernization of Malaysia has caused a increase in supplies and demand, thus creating employment offers, which then attract people to migrate to the city to improve the standard of living. With that comes the increase in the disposable income, this means more money for the family to spend, the new generation of families are getting smaller, most of the young adults who get married are having only one or maximum two kids. All this creates more time and money to be spend for leisure. Here are some factors which contribute to the increase in travel, in and out of Malaysia.

Employee entitled to holiday, creates more free time to be spent doing leisure activities.

More and more companies are practicing a 5 day work week then a 6 day work week, to create a balance.

Increase of living standards result in a larger income, to sustain the cost of living caused by the developing cities.

Families are becoming smaller, younger generation of adults are looking to have one or a maximum of two kids.

With everything becoming more advanced socially, and the cost of living increasing it has come to the point where, there are two earners in one family. This results in more disposable income, due to the small family.

Technology

Besides all that, the advancement in technology also plays an important role in the increase in tourism, computer reservation system has made booking, viewing and making payment easy. Consumers can now view, book and pay for any tourism service without leaving the comfort of their office or their homes.

The Package Tour

The package tour, also called package holiday, also plays a very important role in causing the mass tourism phenomenon. Package travel or all-inclusive package are often standardised and with limited flexibility. The package refers to the purchase of a package of travel services including transport and accommodation. All other types of trips are non-package tours. When buying a package, the tourist feels sure to receive the service promised. the industry tourism has adapted its offer to the customer needs and expectations and proposes tailor-made packages where the customer can combine all the components of his trip. The idea of the package tour is the same but more flexibility is granted.

Effects

The impact of the mass tourism is quite popular, especially upon the environment. Besides, very limited share of money spent on holidays actually get to the local people, which regional and native cultural attractions we all enjoy. These are the people who actually save the traditions and habits of their local areas. The people, who allow us to catch a glimpse of their cultural heritage, they are who have preserving and taking care of the un-spoiled nature for all of us. Maybe many of the people are used to think that big tour operators and large travel consortiums have a responsibility to preserve that local cultural heritage and environment. But they are only concerned about their profit and nothing else. But if one do not look a bit further in future and see that this way, one day there would not be many remaining tourist resources and gains will start descending fast. Unfortunately, this will affect no one so greatly, but the locals. After all, alternative tourism forms include small groups of people, who surely do not harm the environment that much. Besides, one of the aims of the alternative tourism forms is to acknowledge how to preserve the environment and local traditions and culture. Actually, some alternative forms are meant to enable man to appreciate the greatness of nature, a great such example is the eco-tourism. However, it is totally different situation in some big resorts with thousands of people running around and a lot of hotels keeping the beautiful nature views away from your sight. Of course, there are many ways of entertainment in view of the tourist's animation, nightlife, and other. But is it not exactly that what we are running from. Could great nightlife and various animations with the difference they are at different place, compare with the variety of all alternative forms; to compare with the naked nature and cultural heritage.

Advantage

- Jobs are generated by tourism in many areas – in the initial construction of the resorts, in travel, in food provision and in other service related industries.
- Local people benefit directly from employment.
- Transport facilities are developed.
- The local tax base increases so the local government/council can invest in schools, healthcare and social services.

Disadvantage

- TNCs (Trans National Corporations) from rich countries are often involved – this can result in a lot of profits leaving the country.

- Jobs can be seasonal – especially in beach and skiing based resorts. People can therefore find themselves out of work in the close season.
- Tourists consume huge amounts of resources including food and water – this type of tourism is particularly UNSUSTAINABLE in this manner.
- Tourists introduce new values and cultures – this causes cultural pollution.
- Land is lost from farming to tourist developments.

Sustainable Tourism

Sustainable tourism is the concept of visiting somewhere as a tourist and trying to make a positive impact on the environment, society, and economy. Tourism can involve primary transportation to the general location, local transportation, accommodations, entertainment, recreation, nourishment and shopping. It can be related to travel for leisure, business and what is called VFR (visiting friends and relatives). There is now broad consensus that tourism development should be sustainable; however, the question of how to achieve this remains an object of debate.

Without travel there is no tourism, so the concept of sustainable tourism is tightly linked to a concept of sustainable mobility. Two relevant considerations are tourism's reliance on fossil fuels and tourism's effect on climate change. 72 percent of tourism's CO_2 emissions come from transportation, 24 percent from accommodations, and 4 percent from local activities. Aviation accounts for 55% of those transportation CO_2 emissions (or 40% of tourism's total). However, when considering the impact of all greenhouse gas emissions from tourism and that aviation emissions are made at high altitude where their effect on climate is amplified, aviation alone accounts for 75% of tourism's climate impact.

The International Air Transport Association (IATA) considers an annual increase in aviation fuel efficiency of 2 percent per year through 2050 to be realistic. However, both Airbus and Boeing expect the passenger-kilometers of air transport to increase by about 5 percent yearly through at least 2020, overwhelming any efficiency gains. By 2050, with other economic sectors having greatly reduced their CO_2 emissions, tourism is likely to be generating 40 percent of global carbon emissions. The main cause is an increase in the average distance travelled by tourists, which for many years has been increasing at a faster rate than the number of trips taken. "Sustainable transportation is now established as the critical issue confronting a global tourism industry that is palpably unsustainable, and aviation lies at the heart of this issue."

Social and Economic Aspects

Global economists forecast continuing international tourism growth, the amount depending on the location. As one of the world's largest and fastest growing industries, this continuous growth will place great stress on remaining biologically diverse habitats and indigenous cultures, which are often used to support mass tourism. Tourists who promote sustainable tourism are sensitive to these dangers and seek to protect tourist destinations, and to protect tourism as an industry.

Sustainable tourists can reduce the impact of tourism in many ways:

- Informing themselves of the culture, politics, and economy of the communities visited.
- Anticipating and respecting local cultures, expectations and assumptions.
- Supporting the integrity of local cultures by favoring businesses which conserve cultural heritage and traditional values.
- Supporting local economies by purchasing local goods and participating with small, local businesses.
- Conserving resources by seeking out businesses that are environmentally conscious, and by using the least possible amount of non-renewable resources.

Increasingly, destinations and tourism operations are endorsing and following "responsible tourism" as a pathway towards sustainable tourism. Responsible tourism and sustainable tourism have an identical goal, that of sustainable development. The pillars of responsible tourism are therefore the same as those of sustainable tourism – environmental integrity, social justice and economic development. The major difference between the two is that, in responsible tourism, individuals, organizations and businesses are asked to take responsibility for their actions and the impacts of their actions. This shift in emphasis has taken place because some stakeholders feel that insufficient progress towards realizing sustainable tourism has been made since the Earth Summit in Rio. This is partly because everyone has been expecting others to behave in a sustainable manner. The emphasis on responsibility in responsible tourism means that everyone involved in tourism – government, product owners and operators, transport operators, community services, NGOs and Community-based organization (CBOs), tourists, local communities, industry associations – are responsible for achieving the goals of responsible tourism.

Stakeholders

Stakeholders of sustainable tourism play a role in continuing this form of tourism. This can include organizations as well as individuals, to be specific, ECOFIN. "A stakeholder in the tourism industry is deemed to be anyone who is impacted on by development positively or negatively, and as a result it reduces potential conflict between the tourists and host community by involving the latter in shaping the way in which tourism develops.

The Global Sustainable Tourism Council (GSTC) serves as the international body for fostering increased knowledge and understanding of sustainable tourism practices, promoting the adoption of universal sustainable tourism principles and building demand for sustainable travel. It has a number of programmes including the setting of international standards for accreditation agencies (the organisations that would inspect a tourism product, and certify them as a sustainable company).

Governments

The values and ulterior motives of governments often need to be taken into account when assessing the motives for sustainable tourism. One important factor to consider in any ecologically sensitive or remote area or an area new to tourism is that of carrying capacity. This is the capacity of tourists of visitors an area can sustainably tolerate without damaging the environment or culture of the surrounding area. This can be altered and revised in time and with changing perceptions and values. For example, originally the sustainable carrying capacity of the Galapagos Islands was set at 12,000 visitors per annum but was later changed by the Ecuadorian government to 50,000 for economic reasons and objectives.

Non-governmental Organizations

Non-governmental organizations are one of the stakeholders in advocating sustainable tourism. Their roles can range from spearheading sustainable tourism practices to simply doing research. University research teams and scientists can be tapped to aid in the process of planning. Such solicitation of research can be observed in the planning of Cát Bà National Park in Vietnam.

Dive resort operators in Bunaken National Park, Indonesia, play a crucial role by developing exclusive zones for diving and fishing respectively, such that both tourists and locals can benefit from the venture.

Large conventions, meetings and other major organized events drive the travel, tourism and hospitality industry. Cities and convention centers compete to attract such commerce, commerce which has heavy impacts on resource use and the environment. Major sporting events, such as the Olympic Games, present special problems regarding environmental burdens and degradation. But burdens imposed by the regular convention industry can be vastly more significant.

Green conventions and events are a new but growing sector and marketing point within the convention and hospitality industry. More environmentally aware organizations, corporations and government agencies are now seeking more sustainable event practices, greener hotels, restaurants and convention venues, and more energy efficient or climate neutral travel and ground transportation. However, the convention trip not taken can be the most sustainable option: "With most international conferences having hundreds if not thousands of participants, and the bulk of these usually traveling by plane, conference travel is an area where significant reductions in air-travel-related GHG emissions could be made. This does not mean non-attendance", since modern Internet communications are now ubiquitous and remote audio/visual participation. For example, by 2003 Access Grid technology had already successfully hosted several international conferences. A particular example is the large American Geophysical Union's annual meeting, which has used livestreaming for several years. This provides live streams and recordings of keynotes, named lectures and oral sessions, and provides opportunities to submit questions and interact with authors and peers. Following the live-stream, the recording of each session is posted on-line within 24 hours.

Some convention centers have begun to take direct action in reducing the impact of the conventions they host. One example is the Moscone Center in San Francisco, which has a very aggressive recycling program, a large solar power system, and other programs aimed at reducing impact and increasing efficiency.

Local Communities

Local communities benefit from sustainable tourism through economic development, job creation, and infrastructure development. Tourism revenues bring economic growth and prosperity to attractive tourist destinations which can raise the standard of living in destination communities. Sustainable tourism operators commit themselves to creating jobs for local community members. Increase in tourism revenue to an area acts as a driver for the development of increased infrastructure. As tourist demands increase in a destination, a more robust infrastructure is needed to support the needs of both the tourism industry and the local community. A 2009 study of rural operators throughout the province of British Columbia, Canada found "an overall strong 'pro-sustainability' attitude among respondents. Dominant barriers identified were lack of available money to invest, lack of incentive programs, other business priorities, and limited access to suppliers of sustainable products, with the most common recommendation being the need for incentive programs to encourage businesses to become more sustainable."

Sustainable Tourism in Developing Nations

Expansion of Tourism in the LEDCs

The renewed emphasis on outward-orientated growth which accompanied the rise in neoliberal development strategies in the 1990s in the south also focused attention on international tourism as an import potential growth sector for many countries, particularly in Less Economically Developed Countries (LEDCs) as many of the world's most beautiful and 'untouched' places are located in the Third World.

Prior to the 1960s studies tended to assume that the extension of the tourism industry to LEDCs was a good thing. In the 1970s this changed as academics started to take a much more negative view on tourism's consequences, particularly criticising the industry as an effective contributor towards development. International tourism is a volatile industry with visitors quick to abandon destinations that were formerly popular because of threats to health or security.

Problems with Sustainable Tourism in the Third World

Displacement and Resettlement

One common issue with tourism in a place where there was none prior to First World companies arriving is that of the displacement and resettlement of local communities. The Maasai tribes in Tanzania have been a victim of this problem. After the second World War First World conservationists with the intent of making such areas accessible to tourists as well as preserving the areas natural beauty and ecology moved into the areas where the Maasai tribes lived. This was often achieved through the setting up of national parks and conservation areas.

It has been claimed that Maasai activities did not threaten the wildlife and the First World knowledge was blurred by 'colonial disdain' and misunderstandings of savannah wildlife. As the Maasai have been displaced the area within the Ngorongoro Conservation Area (NCA) has been modified to allow easier access for tourists by actions such as building campsites, tracks and the removal of stone objects such as stones for souvenirs.

This kind of 'sustainable tourism' is viewed by many as an oxymoron or metaphor since it seriously can't change anything. There likely is no way to make tourism sustainable but if all tourists cooperate it could possibly work in a viable world. It is a reality that many things done in the name of sustainability are actually masking the desire to allow extra profits. There is often alienation of local populations from the tourists.

Environmental Impacts

"The environmental sustainability focuses on the overall viability and health of ecological systems. Natural resource degradation, pollution, and loss of biodiversity are detrimental because they increase vulnerability, undermine system health, and reduce resilience. This aspect of sustainability has been the most often discussed through the literature by numerous authors such as Hall, C. M. & Lew A.A., Hall, D., Weaver, and many others."

Coastal Tourism

Many coastal areas are experiencing particular pressure from growth in lifestyles and growing numbers of tourists. Coastal environments are limited in extent consisting of only a narrow strip along the edge of the ocean. Coastal areas are often the first environments to experience the detrimental impacts of tourism. A detailed study of the impact on coastal areas, with reference to western India can be an example.

The inevitable change is on the horizon as holiday destinations put more effort into sustainable tourism. Planning and management controls can reduce the impact on coastal environments and ensure that investment into tourism products supports sustainable coastal tourism.

Some studies have led to interesting conceptual models applicable for coastal tourism. The 'inverted funnel model' and the 'embedded model' (Jacob, S. 2008) can be metaphors for understanding the interplay of different stake-holders like government, local community, tourists and business community in developing tourist destinations.

Mountain Tourism

Mount Everest attracts many tourist climbers wanting to summit the peak of the highest mountain in the world each year. Everest is a UNESCO World Heritage site. Over the years, carelessness and excessive consumption of resources by mountaineers, as well as overgrazing by livestock, have damaged the habitats of snow leopards, lesser pandas, Tibetan bears, and scores of bird species. To counteract past abuses, various reforestation programs have been carried out by local communities and the Nepalese government.

Expeditions have removed supplies and equipment left by climbers on Everest's slopes, including hundreds of oxygen containers. A large quantity of the litter of past climbers tons of items such as tents, cans, crampons, and human waste has been hauled down from the mountain and recycled or discarded. However, the bodies of most of the more than 260 climbers who have died on Everest (notably on its upper slopes) have not been removed, as they are unreachable or for those that are accessible their weight makes carrying them down extremely difficult. Notable in the cleanup endeavour have been the efforts of the Eco Everest Expeditions, the first of which was organized in 2008 to commemorate the death that January of Everest-climbing pioneer Sir Edmund Hillary. Those expeditions also have publicized ecological issues (in particular, concerns about the effects of climate change in the region through observations that the Khumbu Icefall has been melting).

Small Island Tourism

Small Islands are especially affected and often depend on tourism, as this industry makes up anywhere from 40% to 75% of the GDP (Gross Domestic Product) for various islands including Barbados, Aruba, Isle of Man, and Anguilla.

Mass tourism tends to put a strain on fragile island ecosystems and the natural resources it provides. Studies have shown that early practices of tourism were unsustainable and took a toll to environmental factors, hurting the natural landscapes that originally drew in the tourists. For example, in Barbados, beaches are the main attraction and have been eroded and destroyed over the years. This is due to inefficient political decisions and policies along with irresponsible tourist activity, such as reckless diving and waste disposal, damaging coastal and marine environments. Such practices also altered physical features of the landscape and caused a loss in biodiversity, leading to the disruption of ecosystems. Many other islands faced environmental damage such as Isle of Man and Samoa.

However, visitors are attracted to the less industrial scene of these islands, and according to a survey by Canavan, over 80% of the people enjoyed the natural landscape when they visited, many commenting that they wanted to protect and save the wildlife in the area. Many tourists have turned to practices of sustainable and eco tourism in attempt to save the nature they enjoy in these locations, while some political entities try to enforce this in attempt to keep tourism in their island afloat.

Sustainable Tourism as Part of a Development Strategy

Third World countries are especially interested in international tourism, and many believe it brings countries a large selection of economic benefits including employment opportunities, small business development, and increased in payments of foreign exchange. Many assume that more money is gained through developing luxury goods and services in spite of the fact that this increases a countries dependency on imported products, foreign investments and expatriate skills. This classic 'trickle down' financial strategy rarely makes its way down to brings its benefits down to small businesses.

It has been said that the economic benefits of large-scale tourism are not doubted but that the backpacker or budget traveller sector is often neglected as a potential growth sector by Third World governments. This sector brings significant non-economic benefits which could help to empower and educate the communities involved in this sector. "Aiming 'low' builds upon the skills of the local population, promotes self-reliance, and develops the confidence of community members in dealing with outsiders, all signs of empowerment" and all of which aid in the overall development of a nation.

Improvements to Sustainable Tourism in the Third World

Management of Sustainable Tourism

There has been the promotion of sustainable tourism practices surrounding the management of tourist locations by locals or the community. This form of tourism is based on the premise that the people living next to a resource are the ones best suited to protecting it. This means that the tourism activities and businesses are developed and operated by local community members, and certainly with their consent and support. Sustainable tourism typically involves the conservation of resources that are capitalized upon for tourism purposes. Locals run the businesses and are responsible for promoting the conservation messages to protect their environment.

Community-based sustainable tourism (CBST) associates the success of the sustainability of the ecotourism location to the management practices of the communities who are directly or indirectly dependent on the location for their livelihoods. A salient feature of CBST is that local knowledge is usually utilised alongside wide general frameworks of ecotourism business models. This allows the participation of locals at the management level and typically allows a more intimate understanding of the environment.

The use of local knowledge also means an easier entry level into a tourism industry for locals whose jobs or livelihoods are affected by the use of their environment as tourism locations. Environmentally sustainable development crucially depends on the presence of local support for a project. It has also been noted that in order for success projects must provide direct benefits for the local community.

However, recent research has found that economic linkages generated by CBST may only be sporadic, and that the linkages with agriculture are negatively affected by seasonality and by the small scale of the cultivated areas. This means that CBST may only have small-scale positive effects for these communities.

It has also been said that partnerships between governments and tourism agencies with smaller communities is not particularly effective because of the disparity in aims between the two groups, i.e. true sustainability versus mass tourism for maximum profit. In Honduras such a divergence can be demonstrated where consultants from the World Bank and officials from the Institute of tourism wanted to set up a selection of 5-star hotels near various ecotourism destinations. But another operating approach in the region by USAID and APROECOH (an ecotourism association) promotes community-based efforts which has trained many local Hondurans. Mader concluded that the grassroot organisations were more successful in Honduras.

Confusion Surrounding Governmental Management of Sustainable Tourism

There has been some discussion regarding the told of inter-governmental organisations and the development of sustainable tourism practices in the third world. In Mowforth and Munt's book 'Tourism and Sustainability: New Tourism in the Third World, they criticised a document that was written by the World Travel and Tourism Council (WTTC), the World Tourism Organisation and the Earth Council, which was included in Agenda 21. It was entitled 'Agenda 21 for the Travel and Tourism Industry: Towards Environmentally Sustainable Development'. Mowforth and Munt commented on the language used to describe the environment and local culture in such documents because the preservation of the environment and local culture are the two main objectives when practising sustainable tourism. They pointed out that some of the key words used were 'core asset', 'core product', 'product quality' and 'preserve'. They argued that the treatment of the environment as a marketable product was clear and that such documents provide a good list of advice for Third World governments regarding sustainable tourism but do not actually provide the resources to incorporate them into the development of their tourism industries.

It is arguments such as these that postulate that there is a gap between the advice given by non-governmental or inter-governmental organisations to Third World governments and what can actually be brought to realisation. These arguments try and persuade readers that documents like the one released by the WTTC that the development of sustainable tourism actually 'bypasses the interests of local people'.

Responsible Tourism

There are many definitions and understandings of responsible tourism. According to the Center for Responsible Tourism, responsible tourism can be defined as, "tourism that maximizes the benefits to local communities, minimizes negative social or environmental impacts, and helps local people conserve fragile cultures and habitats or species." Responsible tourism incorporates not only responsibility with the physical environment, but also an incorporation of awareness for the economic and social interactions whereas, sustainable tourism focuses more on the environmental impacts. Responsible tourism is regarded as a behaviour. It is more than a form of tourism as it represents an approach to engaging with tourism, be that as a tourist, a business, locals at a destination or any other tourism stakeholder. It emphasizes that all stakeholders are responsible for the kind of tourism they develop or engage in. This ensures that the tourism service providers and purchasers or consumers are held accountable. Whilst different groups will see responsibility in different ways, the shared understanding is that responsible tourism should entail an improvement in tourism. Tourism should become 'better' as a result of the responsible tourism approach.

Within the notion of betterment resides the acknowledgement that conflicting interests need to be balanced. However, the objective is to create better places for people to live in and to visit. Importantly, there is no blueprint for responsible tourism: what is deemed responsible may differ depending on places and cultures. Responsible Tourism is an aspiration that can be realized in different ways in different originating markets and in the diverse destinations of the world.

The concept of responsible tourism emerged following the environmental awareness that rose out of the 1960s and 70s amidst a growing phenomenon of "mass tourism". The European Travel Commission in 1973 and a multilateral initiative to instate environmentally sound tourism and development was advanced. The United Nations specialized agency called the World Tourism Organization (UNWTO), highlights the link between tourism and development in aims of achieving the Sustainable Development Goals. Given the dramatic increase in tourism, the report strongly promotes responsible tourism. Given the local based approach of Responsible Tourism, it can also incorporate local populations into the decision making and tourism planning process.

While further research is needed to understand the impacts of responsible tourism, a study conducted in 2017 found that well-managed responsible tourism practices were beneficial to local communities.

Focusing in particular on businesses, according to the Cape Town Declaration on Responsible Tourism, it will have the following characteristics:

- Minimises negative economic, environmental, and social impacts.
- Generates greater economic benefits for local people and enhances the well-being of host communities, improves working conditions and access to the industry.
- Involves local people in decisions that affect their lives and life chances.
- Makes positive contributions to the conservation of natural and cultural heritage, to the maintenance of the world's diversity.
- Provides more enjoyable experiences for tourists through more meaningful connections with local people, and a greater understanding of local cultural, social and environmental issues.
- Provides access for people with disabilities.
- Is culturally sensitive, engenders respect between tourists and hosts, and builds local pride and confidence.

While widely acclaimed, responsible tourism has also been critiqued. Studies have shown that the degree to which individuals engage in responsible tourism is contingent upon their engagement socially. Meaning, tourist behaviors will fluctuate depending on the range of social engagement that each tourist chooses take part in. A study regarding responsible tourists behavior concludes that it is not only a personal behavior of tourists that shape outcomes, but also a reflection of mechanisms put in place by governments. Other research has put into question the promise that tourism even responsible tourism is inline with UN Sustainable Development Goals given the difficulties in measuring such impact. Some argue that actually detracts attention from the wider issues surrounding tourism that are in need of regulation, such as number of visitors and environmental impact.

Humane Tourism

Humane tourism is part of the movement of responsible tourism. The idea is to empower local communities through travel related businesses around the world, first and foremost in developing countries. The idea of humane travel or humane tourism is to connect travelers from Europe, North America, Australia and New Zealand seeking new adventures and authentic experiences directly, to local businesses in the specific locations they wish to visit – thus, giving economic advantages to local businesses and giving travelers authentic and truly unique travel experiences. Humane travel or humane tourism focuses on the people, the local community. The idea is to enable travelers to experience the world through the eyes of its local people while contributing directly to those people, ensuring that tourist dollars benefit the local community directly.

Humane tourism is about giving opportunity to the local people, empower them, enable them to enjoy the fruits of tourism directly. The Internet is changing tourism. More and more travelers are planning their travels and vacations via the net. The Internet enables people to cut off commissions. The traveler can search for new destinations to visit, talk or read about other people experience, and buy the services directly. The Internet platform can encourage local people to start new businesses and that already existing small businesses will begin to promote themselves through the net and receive the economic advantages of this directly in their communities. The world is now in a new tourism age, with globalization and the Internet playing a key role.

The new travelers have traveled the world, they have seen the classic sites. Staying at a Western hotel is not attractive enough, and they are excited by the prospect of experiencing the authentic local way of life: to go fishing with a local fisherman, to eat the fish with his family, to sleep in a typical village house. These tourists or travelers, are happy to know that while doing so they promote the economic well-being of those same people they spend time with.

Humane tourism is part of Responsible tourism. The concept of Responsible Tourism originated in the work of Jost Krippendorf in The Holiday Makers called for "rebellious tourists and rebellious locals" to create new forms of tourism. His vision was "to develop and promote new forms of tourism, which will bring the greatest possible benefit to all the participants – travelers, the host population and the tourist business, without causing intolerable ecological and social damage." As one can see he already talked, back in the 80s about benefits for the host population and used the term human tourism. Humane travel focuses on that host local population.

The South African national tourism policy used the term "responsible tourism" and mentioned the well-being of the local community as a main factor.

The Cape Town Declaration on Responsible Tourism in Destinations, agreed in 2002, that Responsible Tourism is about "making better places for people to live in and better places for people to visit." The declaration focused on "places" but did mention the local population.

From the Rio summit or earth summit on until the UN Commission on Sustainable Development in, the main focus of the tourism industry was the earth, the planet, the places, "green" or "eco" tourism. Now there is a trend to include the local population. This trend or branch of responsible tourism is called humane tourism or humane travel.

Responsible Hospitality

As with the view of responsible tourism, responsible hospitality is essentially about creating better places for people to live in, and better places for people to visit. This does not mean all forms of hospitality are also forms of tourism although hospitality is the largest sector of the tourism industry. As such we should not be surprised at overlaps between responsible hospitality and responsible tourism. In the instance where place of permanent residence is also the place where the hospitality service is consumed, if for example a meal is consumed in a local restaurant, this does not obviate the requirement to improve the place of residence. As such, the essence of Responsible Hospitality is not contingent upon touristic forms of hospitality.

While Friedman famously argued that, admittedly within legal parameters, the sole responsibility of business was to generate profit for shareholders the idea that businesses' responsibility extends beyond this has existed for decades and is most frequently encountered in the concept of corporate social responsibility. There are numerous ways businesses can and do engage in activities that are not intended to benefit shareholders and management, at least not in the short term. However, often acts of corporate social responsibility are undertaken because of the perceived benefit to business. Usually in hospitality this relates to the cost reductions associated with improved energy efficiency but may also relate to, for example, the rise in ethical consumerism and the view that being seen to be a responsible business is beneficial to revenue growth.

As per the Cape Town Declaration on Responsible Tourism, responsible hospitality is culturally sensitive. Instead of then calling for the unachievable, responsible hospitality simply makes the case for more responsible forms of hospitality, hospitality that benefits locals first, and visitors second. Certainly, all forms of hospitality can be improved and managed so that negative impacts are minimized whilst striving for a maximization of positive impacts on the environment.

Experiential Travel

Experiential travel, also known as immersion travel, is a form of tourism in which people focus on experiencing a country, city or particular place by actively and meaningfully engaging with its history, people, culture, food and environment. It can often be transformative. Therewith the concept is based on very similar mechanisms as for example experiential education, experiential knowledge, experiential interior design, and experiential marketing.

Experiential travel can emphasize different areas of local life – culinary, culture, history, shopping, nature or social life – and can therewith be the basis for a holistic travel experience. The goal is to more deeply understand a travel destination's culture, people and history by connecting with it more than just by visiting it. Therefore, the traveller usually gets in touch with locals who give guidance how to experience a place. This can be a friend, an accommodation host or another person.

Experiential travel tends to focus on travel that is inspirational, personalized and/ or creates a path to self-discovery.

The term "experiential travel" is already mentioned in books and publications from 1985 – however it was discovered as a meaningful market trend in 2012. In 2017, 65% of travelers preferred 'experiencing something new' over 'feeling rested and recharged'.

Social Tourism

Social tourism can be defined as "the connections and phenomena related to the participation of people in the countries of destinations as well as of holidaymakers, of disadvantaged layers of society or those unable to participate in tourism, holidays and their advantages for whatever reason".

Social tourism "refers to programmes, events, and activities that enable all population groups – and particularly youth, families, retirees, individuals with modest incomes, and individuals with restricted physical capacity – to enjoy tourism, while also attending to the quality of relations between visitors and host communities".

Concerning the Main Benefits of Social Tourism

- Social tourism is "a shaper of society" as "holidays and travel can provide particularly apt occasions for personal enrichment, through the discovery of new places, cultures and civilizations, through physical, artistic, sport and leisure activities, by meeting people across educational or generation divides, and by other responsibilities taken on freely by tourists."
- Social tourism is a promoter of economic growth: "Tourism for all is a key to economic strength which generates a continuous flow of people and investment, which contributes to regional development."
- Social tourism participates to the regional and local development by "reconciling tourism development, environmental protection and a respect for the identity of local communities".
- Social tourism is a partner in global development programs: "Tourism, when it is controlled and when it respects the natural and cultural environment and local communities, constitutes one of the economic, social and cultural hopes of many developing countries."

Furthermore studies show that social tourism has a tremendous impact on families.

Social tourism was found to increase family capital in the short term, and social capital – in terms of social networks, related pro-active behavior and self-esteem - in the medium term. These increases can be seen as beneficial for the participants and to wider society. Consequently it is suggested that social tourism may be a cost-effective addition to social policy.

The family capital is the relationships between the family members and their resilience when faced with adversity. Both adults and children benefited from an increase in family capital, which could encourage the adults to change parenting techniques and encourage a more active lifestyle for the family (for example, going out more). For the children this could lead to better behaviour both at home and at school.

The raise of the social capital of is the increase of the valuable relations between the individual and the world surrounding him or her. Ways in which an increase in social capital can manifest itself include improvements in self-confidence, extension of support networks, new ways of prioritizing duties, changes in work circumstances, and better budgeting skills.

Its actions are based on the belief that holidays benefit individuals as well as wider society because they:

- Improve well-being and reduce stress.
- Increase self-esteem and confidence.
- Strengthen family communication and bonding.
- Provide new skills, widen perspectives and enhance employability.
- Give long-lasting, treasured memories.
- Result in happier, stronger families and a more inclusive society.

Dark Tourism

Dark tourism (also black tourism or grief tourism) has been defined as tourism involving travel to places historically associated with death and tragedy. More recently, it was suggested that the concept should also include reasons tourists visit that site, since the site's attributes alone may not make a visitor a "dark tourist". The main attraction to dark locations is their historical value rather than their associations with death and suffering.

Murambi Technical School where many of the murders in the Rwandan genocide took place is now a genocide museum.

The Catacombs have become a popular site for thanatourism, and guided tours are frequently held in small areas of the complex of tunnels and chambers.

Field of Study

While there is a long tradition of people visiting recent and ancient settings of death, such as travel to gladiator games in the Roman colosseum, attending public executions by decapitation, and visiting the catacombs, this practice has been studied academically only relatively recently. Travel writers were the first to describe their tourism to deadly places. P. J. O'Rourke called his travel to Warsaw, Managua, and Belfast in 1988 'holidays in hell', or Chris Rojek talking about 'black-spot' tourism in 1993 or the 'milking the macabre'.

Academic attention to the subject originated in Glasgow, Scotland: The term 'dark tourism' was coined in 1996 by Lennon and Foley, two faculty members of the Department of Hospitality, Tourism & Leisure Management at Glasgow Caledonian University, and the term 'thanatourism' was first mentioned by A. V. Seaton in 1996, then Professor of Tourism Marketing at the University of Strathclyde.

As of 2014, there have been many studies on definitions, labels, and subcategorizations, such as Holocaust tourism and slavery-heritage tourism, and the term continues to be molded outside academia by authors of travel literature. There is very little empirical research on the perspective of the dark tourist. Dark tourism has been formally studied from three main perspectives by a variety of different disciplines.

Hospitality and Tourism

Scholars in this interdisciplinary field have examined many different aspects. Lennon and Foley expanded their original idea in their first book, deploring that "tact and taste do not prevail over economic considerations" and that the "blame for transgressions cannot lie solely on the shoulders of the proprietors, but also upon those of the tourists, for without their demand there would be no need to supply."

Criticism

The Exploitation of the Deceased

Whether a tourist attraction is educational or exploitative is defined by both its operators and its visitors. Tourism operators motivated by greed can "milk the macabre" or reexamine tragedies for a learning experience. Tourists consuming dark tourism products may desecrate a place and case studies are needed to probe who gains and loses.

Thanatourism and slum-tourism have been described as re-interpreting the pastime according to the needs of financial elite.

Misinformation

Chris Hedges described the "Alcatraz narrative as presented by the National Park Service" as "whitewashing", because it "ignores the savagery and injustice of America's system of mass incarceration". By omitting challenging details, the park service furthers a "Disneyfication", per Hedges.

Example of Destinations

Destinations of dark tourism include: Castles and battlefields such as Culloden in Scotland and Bran Castle and Poienari Castle in Romania; former prisons such as Beaumaris Prison in Anglesey, Wales and the Jack the Ripper exhibition in the London Dungeon; sites of natural disasters or man made disasters, such as Hiroshima Peace Memorial Park in Japan, Chernobyl in Ukraine and the commercial activity at Ground Zero in New York one year after September 11, 2001. It also includes sites of human atrocities and genocide, such as the Auschwitz concentration camp in Poland, the Nanjing Massacre Memorial Hall in China, the Tuol Sleng Genocide Museum in Cambodia; the sites of the Jeju Uprising in South Korea and the Spirit Lake Internment Camp Centre near La Ferme, Quebec as an example of Canada's internment operations of 1914–1920.

In Bali "death and funeral rites have become commodified for tourism, where enterprising businesses begin arranging tourist vans and sell tickets as soon as they hear someone is dying." In the US, visitors can tour the Holocaust Memorial Museum in Washington D.C. "with an identity card which matches their age and gender with that of a name and photo of a real holocaust victim. Against a backdrop of video interpretation portraying killing squads in action, the pseudo holocaust victim enters a personal ID into monitors as they wander around the attraction to discover how their real-life counterpart is faring."

Educational Tourism

Educational tourism also called as edu-tourism is a sub type of the travel and tourism sector. Educational tourism could be referred to as an approach for pursuing education, carrying out research activities and knowledge acquisition. This sector is acquiring popularity these days and is a fast growing sub-sector in the travel and tourism industry. As far as academics are concerned, this sector has vast scope and is changing the dynamics of the sector constantly; it is more of a perspective type of tourism. Educational tourism is also called by other names such as job development, career enhancement or self-actualisation experience. The idea is that apart from selfimprovement, travel can be relaxation, learning can be more fun than ever and there is no age bar restricting people from learning by travelling (this does not include people who wish to travel for educational purposes but are unable to travel due to health problems).

Educational cruises, school trips, seminar vacations, study abroad experiences and self enhancement vacations are few examples of educational tourism. Knowledge can be imparted in a much better manner apart from sitting in one corner and reading books. Practicality is far better than theory. Educational tourism does not depend upon weather; a proper infrastructure should be in place and you are good to go! The main focus is to apply the knowledge and skills learnt within the classroom environment in a totally diverse environment, like the "International Practicum Training Program". The structure of educational tourism recognises three aspects the science of tourism, the most popular from of educational tourism. It helps in developing a scientific approach towards the world and a responsible and conscious attitude towards nature and the environment.

The current scenario of education is on a better scale. The concept of informal learning is more appreciated than formal learning. The increasing awareness and importance of education is driving the education industry towards growth. New education styles, new information and research techniques and good exposure to science has enabled the growth of the educational scenario across the world. This is the main aspect that fuels the growth of the educational tourism sector, owing to the advantages of "education with travel". The thirst for knowledge has also increased thereby encouraging people to travel across the globe to gain knowledge of different concepts and technologies that they had studied earlier. This propels the spread of educational tourism across the world. Moreover, individuals try to enhance their technical knowhow and competency outside the classroom environment. They opt for travelling to other regions, meeting people with experience and knowledge and grasping information as and when possible. This adds to the growth of the educational tourism sector.

Educational tourism generally involves study tours. In the tourism industry, it is considered as the most advanced form of travel. This can be attributed to knowledge acquisition and skills enhancement. Lifelong learning, learning with fun and selfimprovement are the common aspects between the "many" forms of educational tourism. The various forms or new trends in educational tourism include school excursions, student exchange programs, senior seminars and environmental tourism.

Challenges

For every gain there is always a spend associated with it. Despite being a fast growing sector in the tourism industry, there are certain challenges that could limit the spread of the educational tourism sector. Political changes can have adverse effects on this sector. Moreover, a bigger challenge is to maintain the quality of education and learning, the involvement of high costs needed for the establishment of research facilities and lack of government support. The sole purpose of this type of tourism is to give equal chance to people of any age, religion, class or society/nationality.

United States can be given the first rank with regards to education as it provides and strives to maintain the best educational facilities, encourages educational tours and spends on quality learning and research. United Kingdom comes second followed by Australia. Germany, France and Japan are also excelling in the educational tourism sector, but they face a major common problem – the language barrier. Developing countries have shown reasonable growth in this sector.

Global travel companies anticipate a lucrative growth in the educational tourism sector. Though nascent in certain areas of the world, many travel companies are conducting educational tours, thereby promoting the importance of education and contributing to the growth of the educational tourism sector. Companies are emphasising on student enhancement through educational tours by imparting technical as well as environmental knowledge.

The educational tourism sector might become a big educational paradigm, adding value to the society by increasing the level of education and generating new economic opportunities. Educational tourism will also give equal chance to the ageing population as education has no barriers with respect to age. The content of educational tours and expeditions should necessarily be subject oriented and result oriented providing people with a full knowledge pack.

Craft Beer Tourism

Craft beer tourism refers to tourism where the primary motivation of travel is to visit a brewery, beer festival, beer related activity or other event that allows attendees to experience all aspects of the craft beer-making, consuming and purchasing process. Travel and tourism constitute one of the largest industries in the world, with Americans spending a total of $1.1 trillion in domestic and international travel in 2018. The beer tourism industry has evolved from the larger culinary and beverage tourism category in which people began planning travels based around experiencing food and drink of different geographies. Informally, vacations centric to the theme of enjoying beer have been dubbed “beercations”.

The theory behind beer tourism is that people want to feel more connected to the beer that they are drinking. People have always been traveling to explore different cultures, geographies and even foods. Tourism within the beverage industry has long seen success with the development of enotourism-tourism related to the wine consumption and making process. Regions such as Northern California, and Tuscany have seen a large influx of tourists whose soul purpose is to sample the regions’ wine. Beer tourism has seen an increase in recent years due to the rising popularity of craft beer and increased prevalence of microbreweries. In a study done by Nielsen it is reported that the average American has visited 2.1 breweries in the last year while traveling. The cultural movement of neolocalism, a movement aimed at preserving the identity of a community and promoting aspects that make it cultural unique, is stimulating this surge in microbrewery success. People want to purchase and consume products that are tied to the geography in which they are located. A study investigating the factors of the craft beer success found that the factor that communities found most important in establishing brand loyalty was the connection that the brewery had to the local community. This brings an explanation to the names, logos and imagery that are tied to the local geography in so many brewing establishments. Microbreweries are also said to be “hyper-local” in the sourcing of their ingredients, sourcing ingredients from their local communities to reflect the product of the local geography and give their beer even more local character. Colorado based, Crooked Stave Brewery, uses locally sourced fruits such as peaches and apricots in all of their flavored beers; similarly, Yazoo Brewing in Nashville, Tennessee uses locally sourced honey as a sweetener in each of it’s flagship beers. In pushing this emphasis on local flavor, and geography differentiated experiences, breweries are giving tourists a reason to explore their products and facilities as a facet of their travel.

Many cities throughout the country have benefitted from the brewery tourism industry. The craft beer industry contributed $79 billion to the United States economy and was responsible for 559,545 jobs in 2018 alone. Some cities have emerged as popular beercation destinations for travelers.

Denver, Colorado

Advertisement for Denver Based “Buds and Brew” Tour.

Denver, Colorado is a city that is has a long track record of success when it comes to brewing dating back to 1873 and the establishment of Coors Brewing Company. Denver is home to 72 breweries, and over 150 breweries when including its surrounding suburbs. This is the most of any metro area in America. Along with the sheer number of Breweries, Denver, also has long been a hub for beer making and tasting. Denver hosts America's largest beer festival, The Great American Beer Festival, which is held every year in Denver and is hosted by the Brewery Association of America which is headquartered in nearby Boulder, Colorado. The Great American Beer Fest was visited by over 90,000 people, 800 breweries were represented and over 4,000 different beers were showcased in 2019. Denver also offers a "Buds and Brews" beer and cannabis tour that allows tourists to explore both the flourishing cannabis and craft beer scene in Denver. Denver's RiNo District, River North, is a neighborhood in northern Denver, described as Denver's arts district, that is home to many different craft breweries over a small area. Popular stops on a Denver, Colorado brewery trip are Great Divide Brewing, River North Brewery and Wynkoop Brewing Company.

Portland, Oregon

Beer flight.

Portland, Oregon is a medium sized west coast city that is home to over 70 breweries within its city limits. Portland's craft beer scene is considered by many to be the most impressive of any in America. With such an impressive craft beer and brewing scene the city of Portland, Oregon has been nicknamed "Beervana". Oregon has over 19 million visitors to the state who attributed a portion of their vacation to visiting a brewery, more than any other state in the United States. Oregon is also the second largest producer of Hops in the United States; 15% of the total U.S. Hop production. The Oregon brewing industry continues to support job growth in the state, employing roughly 31,000 Oregonians, and contributing $4.49 billion to the state's economy. The craft beer industry added around 1,340 jobs between 2014 and 2016, a growth of nearly 22 percent. Unique to Portland's beer scene is Zwickelmania which is a weekend long open house that allows tourists free access to all the sites in all of the breweries in the city. Portland even has a hotel specially designed for beer vacationers called the Kennedy School Hotel which is built inside an old brewery. Portland's inner-southeast district has emerged as a popular stop for beer drinkers. The neighborhood was once the industrial center of the city, but the industry has given way to a growing art scene, and abandoned factories and warehouses are being converted into restaurants and brewing operations. Frequented stops on a Portland, Oregon "beercation" are Cascade Barrelhouse, Level Brewing, and Ecliptic Brewery.

Portland, Maine

Portland, Maine is a small city in northern New England. With a population of only 66,882 people, Portland has the most breweries per capita of any city in America at 25 breweries per 100,000 residents. This coastal city is best known for its seafood and great beaches, but it is also now recognized as the beer capital of New England. The New England Craft Beer Summit is hosted every year in Portland, Maine. The weekend is highlighted by educational workshops for Brewers looking to open a businesses as well as tastings and activities for visitors to come an explore beer from across New England. Portland remains a very small city in terms of area which means that beer travelers enjoy the luxury of ease of access being able to walk to a high number of breweries in a small radius. Portland's arts district located on the north-eastern edge of the city is clustered with outdoor theaters, coffee shops, and brewing operations including the famed Shipyard Brewing Company. Converted warehouses house different brewing operations, many of them even under the same roof. In 2017 alone 9 million tourists to the city of Portland, Maine visited a brewery, 1 in 5 tourists. Frequented stops on a Portland, Maine beercation include, Bissell Brothers Brewing Company, Allagash Brewing, and Novares Bier Cafe.

Activities

Facility Tours

Brewery tour.

Facility tours are interactive experiences in which visitors of a brewery are guided through the facilities of the brewery by either a tour guide or beer maker. Visitors are educated on the different processes in a brewery from canning and bottling to the fermentation process. Tour guides will often explain the history of the brewery highlighting certain aspects of the breweries founding, and the tours sometimes come with a complimentary tasting. Dog Fish Head's facility tour in Milton, Delaware costs $30 per tour and tour-goers are given complete access to the facility, and are gifted with a complimentary tasting and souvenir beer glass.

City Brewery Tours

City Brewery tours differ city to city and tour company to tour company, but the general premise remains the same. Tour companies set up tours with local beer makers and breweries that allow for patrons of the tour to receive free samples and tastings at different breweries with the price of admission for the tour. Tours also usually offer transportation between locations, some provide transport via bus, others include organized biking or walking tours. Many tours may also be paired with food from a local restaurant. BeerQuest Beer Tours in downtown Portland, Oregon offers both a walking and biking tour, and even include seasonal holiday and haunted pub crawls as well. Tapped Enterprises in Long Island, New York offers a Bay Brews, and Fishing Cruise Tour, which includes stops at local breweries, finished off with an afternoon of Flounder fishing in Long Island Sound.

Beer Gardens

Taxisgarten, a traditional beer garden.

A beer garden is an outdoor area where beer and local food is served. The areas are typically surrounded by trees or green space giving them the "garden" portion of their name. Beer gardens are traditionally accompanied by live local music and seating is communal featuring long tables and benches to facilitate conversation. Rising Tide Brewing in Portland, Maine features a beer garden and during weekends in the summer they have live music, local food trucks and even local farm vendors. Beer gardens trace their roots back to Germany where early brewers were forced by law to brew their beer in summer months, and because of the heat they stored their beer underground in cellars to keep it cool, and because of this, drinking the beer on the premises where it was stored resulted in outdoor beer gardens.

Infrastructure to Support Growth

There are important political and economic infrastructure that has been in place that supports the growth of the beer and brewing industry. The craft brewing industry has benefitted from a recent break on excise tax levied on alcohol producers. Microbreweries fall under the "craft beverage" distinction which gives beer producers the benefits of a lower tax on the beer produced to $16 per barrel on the first six million barrels brewed and lowered it to $3.50 per barrel for small brewers on the first 60,000 barrels produced domestically. In addition to the tax benefit, Microbreweries have also gained more power in state politics with the establishment of state brewing guilds and associations. These organizations serve as a unified voice for all breweries within a state. They operate to lobby for the protections necessary to fairly license, regulate, tax, distribute and enforce the legal sale of beer in a safe and beneficial way within their communities. Brewers Guilds also often host festivals, or city and state "brewery weeks" to bring attention to the local beer businesses. In 2018 it was reported that every state in the United States had some form of brewing guild, association or group that could represent the brewing community in state-wide matters. Ability to self-distribute is also an important factor in the continued growth of craft brewery success. In 36 out of 50 states craft breweries are able to distribute directly to consumers using their own distribution channels which allows for brewers to obtain higher gross margin and not have to rely on existing distribution channels. This also allows for tourists to come directly to a brewery and purchase beer to bring home with them instead of hoping that a local retailer carries the beer. There is significant push-back from local government in many states on this issue.

Online Applications and Social Media

Untappd Smartphone App Logo.

The beer and brewing industry as with any other has developed a following online in the form of social media. Multiple websites and social media applications have established platforms that allow for the sharing, recommending and reviewing of local beers and breweries. Beeradvocate.com has emerged as "the go to resource for beer" and allows users to rank, share, and review beers of different beer makers across the world. Beeradvocate also has a ranking feature that compiles a list of reviews from all of its users to rank that the total cumulative score of beers by its users. Untappd is another beer sharing application that promotes the tourism of beer and breweries. Untappd is an app for iOS and Android devices that allows users to rate, review and comment on beers and breweries. The app allows users to tag certain friends and post pictures and "check-in" at local bars and breweries to let their friends know they are trying a new beer.

Beer Tourism Index

In 2015 the popular travel and accommodation booking website, Travelocity.com, conducted a survey on to their users aimed at exploring the purpose for their users travel. When a substantial portion of the survey respondents indicated that visiting a brewery or sampling local beer was a reason for their travel, the website decided to established the first 'Beer Tourism Index' that is used to rank metro areas throughout the United States on how conducive the destination is to a good "beercation". The Index ranked cities based on four main criteria, the prevalence of breweries, availability of rideshare services, accessibility via air, and the average cost of lodging.

Agritourism

Agritourism or agrotourism, as it is defined most broadly, involves any agriculturally based operation or activity that brings visitors to a farm or ranch. Agritourism has different definitions in different parts of the world, and sometimes refers specifically to farm stays, as in Italy. Elsewhere, agritourism includes a wide variety of activities, including buying produce direct from a farm stand, navigating a corn maze, slopping hogs, picking fruit, feeding animals, or staying at a bed and breakfast (B&B) on a farm. Agritourism activities fall within at least one of the five categories of agritourism, and they may span multiple categories. The five categories are: direct-to-consumer sales (e.g., farmstands, u-pick), agricultural education (e.g., school visits to a farm), hospitality (overnight farm stays), recreation (e.g., hunting, horseback riding), and entertainment (e.g., hayrides, harvest dinners).

A lodging cottage.

Agritourism is a form of niche tourism that is considered a growth industry in many parts of the world, including Australia, Canada, the United States, and the Philippines. Other terms associated with agritourism are "agritainment", "value added products", "farm direct marketing" and "sustainable agriculture".

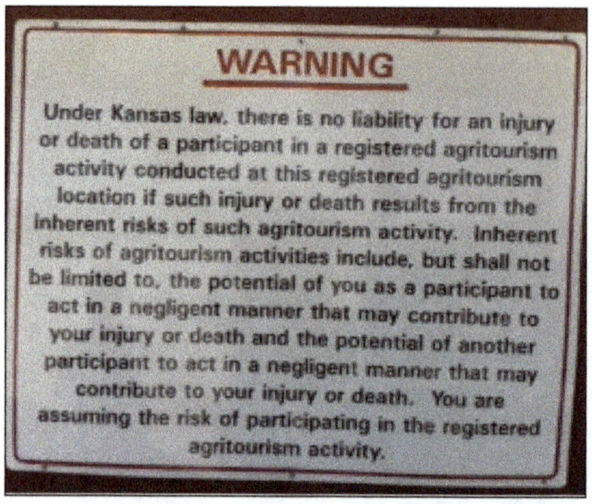

Sign disclaiming legal responsibility at a Kansas agritourism business.

Rural building.

Public Awareness

People have become more interested in how their food is produced. They want to meet farmers and processors and talk with them about what goes into food production. For many people who visit farms, especially children, the visit marks the first time they see the source of their food, be it a dairy cow, an ear of corn growing in a field, or an apple they can pick right off a tree.

Farmers and ranchers use this interest to develop traffic at their farm or ranch, and interest in the quality of their products, as well as awareness of their products.

Safety

While revenue and education are often primary drivers for farmers to diversify and invite guests onto their property, safety isn't always a top priority. Accidents involving tractors, wagon rides, trips, falls, and traffic occur at agritourism operations on a regular basis. Data and specific cases of agrotourism-related injuries are tracked and stored by researchers and scientists. Some of this data is available at publicly accessible sites such as AgInjuryNews.org.

Economic Benefits

Agricultural tourism has become a necessary means for many small farms' survival. By diversifying business operations, farm operators are able to ensure a more stable income. This is because agritourism activities can occur during times of the year that crops may not be in season, and by providing a completely separate stream of income. Some studies have found that agritourism operations often benefit their surrounding communities by drawing tourists to the area. The economic boost by the increase in traffic can be beneficial to rural areas in need of diversified streams of income.

Agrotourism in Various Countries

Agrotourism in Latvia is a popular international tourist destination with many farming tours available such as grain, vegetable, fruit, dairy, and livestock. The farms display the lifestyles and work of active farmers, farming processes, farm products, and the opportunities and positive aspects of a life in the countryside. Tourists can learn how food is made from the field to the final product whilst also engaging in harvesting if possible. Some tours focus on traditional local Latvian cuisine such as cottage cheese, buckwheat, seaberry buckthorn, caraway cheese, dark rye bread and cured meats. Brewing beer is also widely popular with plenty of breweries producing a wide array of beer types. In addition, farms are gaining popularity that promote and teaches the way Latvian's traditionally used to live and farm their produce.

The country-hotel scene has come on apace since 1960, when the Michelin guide to Italy listed not a single establishment in the Chianti area. But even after the boom in rural accommodation in the 1970s, 1980s and 1990s, the choice was still limited, by and large, to basic agroturismo farm-holiday places or rather stuffy country-house hotels. The past few years have seen the arrival of a handful of stylish luxury spa resorts, and some mid-range options where guests benefit from a hands-on, personal approach.

Since 1985 agritourism in Italy is formally regulated by a state law, emended in 2006. The law states basic requirements to claim the title of "agriturismo", and delegates single regions to further regulate the matter.

Italian agritourism attract visitors from all around the globe. In particular, given the luxury nature of rural tourism, international flows are demand-driven.

In the province of Hatay, The village of Vakifli has a small eco and cultural tourism industry, as it is often touted as the last rural village in Turkey where Armenians live. The small village has a guest house where visitors can buy organic products and see the life of the village. There is potential for ecotourism in the Aegean area of Western Turkey as well, and is a growing industry there.

Agritourism is widespread in the United States. Agritourists can choose from a wide range of activities that include picking fruits and vegetables, riding horses, tasting honey, learning about wine and cheesemaking, or shopping in farm gift shops and farm stands for local and regional produce or hand-crafted gifts.

According to the USDA Cooperative State, Education and Extension Service, "Tourism is becoming increasingly important to the U.S. economy. A conservative estimate from the Federal Reserve Board in Kansas, based on 2000 data, shows that basic travel and tourism industries accounted for 3.6 percent of all U.S. employment. Even more telling, data from the Travel Industry Association of America indicate that 1 out of every 18 people in the U.S. has a job directly resulting from travel expenditures."

A herb farm.

Through the Small Farm Center at the University of California, "Agricultural tourism or agritourism, is one alternative for improving the incomes and potential economic viability of small farms and rural communities. Some forms of agritourism enterprises are well developed in California, including fairs and festivals. Other possibilities still offer potential for development". The UC Small Farm Center has developed a California Agritourism Database that "provides visitors and potential entrepreneurs with information about existing agritourism locations throughout the state."

Promoting Tourism in Rural America explains the need for planning and marketing a rural community and weighing the pros and cons of tourism. According to the publication, local citizen participation is helpful and should be included in starting any kind of a tourism program. Citizen participation in planning tourism can contribute to building a successful program that enhances the community. Additional websites that promote and publicize agritourism in the United States include Rural Bounty, founded by agritourism consultant Jane Eckert, Farm Stay U.S., a nationwide directory of farm stays, and The Farm Stay Project, a blog that profiles farm stays and tracks agritourism news.

The UK has seen an increase in Agro tourism as farmers diversify their income streams. Attractions range from accommodation on farms to dedicated farm parks where visitors can interact with animals, attend talks and children can take part in farm based play. Farm parks are sometimes small petting zoos in cities whilst others are areas within working farms set aside as areas for the public. The UK has an industry group for Agro tourism called National Farm Attractions Network who issue best practice information and certification to members.

In the county of Cornwall there are many Agro tourism attractions including the petting zoo at Land's End, Dairy world in New quay and Healey's Cornish Cyder Farm near the capital Truro.

Dude Ranches

Dude (or guest) ranches offer tourists the chance to work on cattle ranches, and sometimes participate in cattle drives.

The fact sheet, *Promoting the Farm and Ranch Recreation Business*, gives farmers and ranchers information on marketing and developing strategies to win tourism dollars. Dude ranches are common in the United States and Australian Outback.

Creative Tourism

Creative tourism has been stimulated as new form of tourism by more skilled forms of tourism activities, by the growth of new consumption patterns, and by changes in the production of tourism products. It can solve that problems experienced by tourists in the conventional tourism. Creativity has many definitions and that based on the function of creativity, it was historically related to creative person, but the recent research in creativity focused on creative product. However, creativity can be located in four areas, and they are: Creative person, creative product, creative process, and creative environment. Creativity means "the production of novel and useful ideas in any domain", which refers to the generation of ideas. creativity becomes as a strategy that promoting individual skill development and innovation, this strategy has been followed by many cities and regions around the world in order to obtain the growth throughout commodification, knowledge development, globalization and increasing competition. Creativity can play a significant role in the mainstream tourism experiences that can be added to the places' atmosphere, creativity is considered as an attractive policy for stimulating other creative activities and outcomes of social, economic and cultural through spilling knowledge and networking. Indeed, creativity can impact tourism in many ways such as: tourism itself as a creative area, tourism products, skills development and performance development. Thus, the important role of creativity in tourism has been incarcerated in many trends.

Tourism is often considered as one of the creative industries, and therefore many destinations around the world have been applied 'creative tourism' in their location. 'Creative tourism' can be defined as "tourism which offers visitors the opportunity to develop their creative potential through active participation in courses and learning experiences which are characteristic of the holiday destination where they are undertaken". This could include some of the more active forms of special interest tourism such as cookery, painting, photography, crafts and arts holidays. Creative tourism is being pursued particularly by those destinations which cannot compete on the basis of their resources. Applying creativity in tourism can take place in the four areas, for example: involving creative person in creative activities, using creative tourism products as attractions, utilizing creative process in providing tourists with creative activities and using creative environment for visiting creative clusters. Thus, creative tourism has become as a significant tool for developing specific environment experience by producing innovative and more flexible tourism's forms, by developing creative tourism production, and by repackaging tourist services. Creative production in tourism has been stimulated by the nature of tourism itself, and by increasing the attractiveness of creative occupations.

The development of creative production can be stimulated by creative industries strategies. Other creative city strategies can be used to foster creativity among citizens to obtain creative cities. Tourism is one of creative industries, and therefore tourism can be developed by creative industries that aim to enhance destinations' image. Tourism links to creativity through a number of creative activities in destinations that can create 'special interest tourists' or tourists consuming creative performances. Thus, the destination itself in creative tourism needs to be more creative through designing the distinctive features of destination experiences, and therefore the destination needs to select the right creativity' s aspects that are related to place, this can create a specific motivation among creative tourists to visit that place. Each place has the ability to provide a unique combination of skills, social capital, knowledge, atmosphere and physical assets, this combination can make a certain place as a uniqueness and suitable destination for specific creative activities or particular creative tradition. Many of creative tourists with specific interests can be attracted to the 'creative destination'.

The strategies of creative tourism have been implemented in destinations that classified as fully conventional tourism. Tourism creative approaches can be linked to several strategies, which help tourism to create distinctive destinations by promoting for creative cities; creative class and creative industries. Creativity can provide atmosphere, activity and content for tourism, which in turn supports a number of creative activities. Increasing integration between creativity and tourism is a significant indicator that tourism is a creative industry. Thus, creative tourism involves 'authentic' experiences and co-creation of participative. More specific creative tourism has been initiated in many places such as artistic havens in rural regions and major cities. The conclusion, creative tourism can be considered as one of development tools in tourism, it is also an alternative of conventional tourism and more specifically mass tourism. Creative tourism consists of a number of creative practices including place, production and consumption. Thus, creative tourism involves the creative interactions of policy makers, producers, landscapes and consumers in order to build creativity in tourism experiences.

3

Cultural Tourism

Tourism that aims to explore the cultural aspects of any region comes under cultural tourism. Some of the example include archaeological tourism, holocaust tourism, dracula tourism, heritage tourism, music tourism, pop-culture tourism, literary tourism, etc. The topics elaborated in this chapter will help in gaining a better perspective about different types of cultural tourism.

Cultural tourism, arguably, is regarded as the original form of tourism considering its roots in the Grand Tour originated in the 16th century in Britain. However, trying to define this concept is more challenging as it may sound; this complex concept may have different meaning for different people. McKercher and Du Cros discuss 'the number of definitions for cultural tourism nearly matches the number of cultural tourists". According to a study conducted by European Commission regarding habits of cultural consumption for Europeans in 2002, people tend to visit galleries and museums abroad as frequently as they do at their homes. Although this issue highlights an emerging concern for cultural activities, it also manifests a contradiction regarding the difference between cultural tourism and cultural visits taken place at home. In general, cultural tourism may be explained as the very nature of travelling in order to understand and become familiar with way of life and history of a specific location accompanied by a range of cultural factors which can be presented in the context of tourism, these factors may include the food, entertainment, architecture, drink, hand crafted and manufactured products or every element representing characteristics of way of life in a particular destination. In addition, several non-cultural and non-educational activities may provide opportunities for familiarizing tourist with each other in a destination. Furthermore, the ongoing debates regarding the effects of cultural tourism on societies and the culture itself introduce another issue where promoting this 'potential source of tourism growth' will actually contribute to communities in terms of cultural and environmental values or 'penetrate sensitive cultural environments' and eventually diminish the very identity of destinations. As Butler (1990) argues; 'although cultural tourists are usually seen as 'good' tourists who travel in small numbers and do little damage, they can arguably act as the 'Trojan Horse' that opens up a region to the less acceptable effects of mass tourism".

Therefore, it is not easy to provide a definite framework which demonstrates the importance and significance of cultural tourism and tourists in general or for a particular destination. Accordingly, defining the problematic concept of cultural tourism brings about a number of issues. One the most important issue lies within defining the two consisting elements of cultural tourism; 'culture' and 'tourism', which both, in their own terms, are difficult to explain. Majority of the available definitions for cultural tourism 'agree that it consists of the consumption of culture by tourists', however Richards argues defining this concept from this perspective reveals a number of fundamental questions;

- What kinds of culture should be included within the scope of cultural tourism?
- Does a visit to a museum turn an entire holiday into a cultural tourism experience?
- Are tourists who engage in cultural consumption actually culturally motivated?

In order to clearly define the concept of cultural tourism it is first necessary to have a basic understanding of the two complex definitions of culture and tourism. However, it should be noted that recognizing the two concepts of culture and tourism separately is considered as a prerequisite for defining cultural tourism. The definition of cultural tourism itself is quite different and should not be assumed as a combination of the meanings of these two terms, culture and tourism.

Tourism

Comparing to the broad concept of culture, tourism is perhaps an easier term to deal with. The known definitions of tourism is divided into two categorizes; the 'conceptual' definition of tourism, dealing with the core meaning of tourism, and the 'technical' definition of tourism, focused on evaluating and measuring the value of tourism which is particularly variable in different countries. These two categorizes are briefly explained in Figure below.

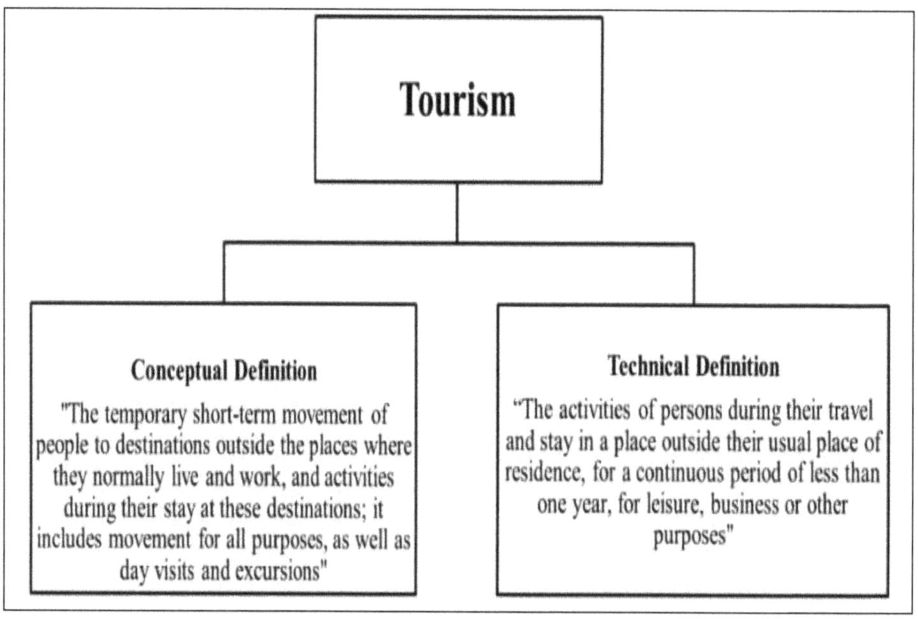

Conceptual and technical definitions of tourism.

Culture

Culture is a very complex concept; hundreds of definitions for it are in literatures. Generally, 'culture' is viewed as a 'complex whole, which delivers a unifying concept for the extensively varied ways of life." 'Trying to describe 'culture' in a single broadly acceptable definition therefore produces a level of generalization which renders the act of definition useless." Two available uses of this concept in literature, culture as 'process' and culture as 'product', are described below.

Concept of Culture in Literature

Culture	
As 'process'	As 'product'
Derived from anthropology and sociology which regard culture mainly as codes of conduct embedded in a specific social group, culture designates the social field of meaning production, or the process through which people make sense of themselves and their lives.	Derives Particularly from literary criticism. Culture is regarded as the product of individual or group activities to which certain meanings are attached, thus 'high 'culture might be used by some to refer to the products of famous artists, whereas 'low' culture might refer to TV soap programs.

In the field of tourism, these two distinctive approaches seem to slightly overlap and integrate. In other words, tourism, accompanied by other social mechanism, may act as a catalyst to transform culture as process into culture as product, thus isolating and detaching cultural products from their initial social context. As mentioned before, this issue poses a challenge in defining the creditability of cultural tourism in the first place.

Although understanding different definitions of culture and its role in society may easily reveal its relation to tourism, it would be unwise and needless to explain them in this topic. Ashworth categorized three definitions of culture related to tourism shown in figure. The first one and the most limited definition is aesthetic productivity. Regarded as 'Art Tourism', this is the simplest form of culture to be commodified for tourism, generally associated with art and artistic products and performance; i.e., theater, ballet, concert, festivals, museums and opera performances (Ashworth, 1995). The second definition of culture is mentioned as 'Heritage Tourism', most manifested in a mix of preserved buildings, conserved cityscapes and morphological patterns, as well as places associated with historical events and personalities. The last and the most general of the three definitions of culture mentioned by Ashworth is 'Place-specific Tourism', 'meaning that culture can be defined as the common set of values, attitudes and thus behavior of a social group'.

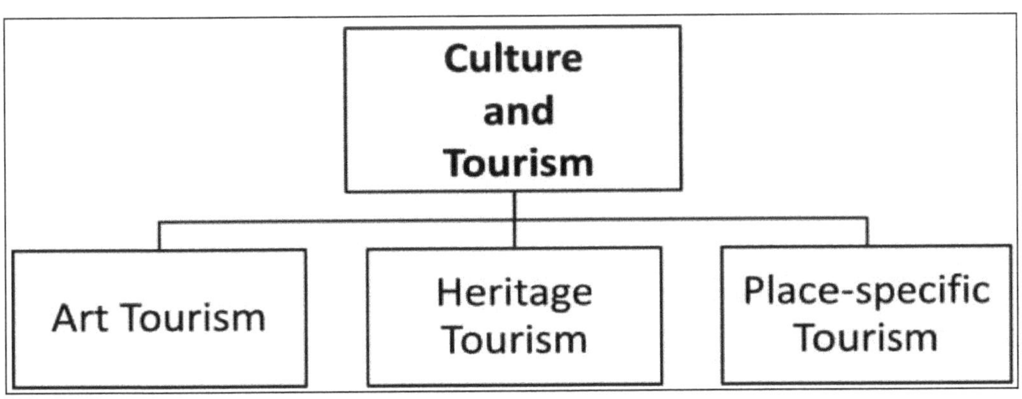

Definitions of culture related to tourism.

Typology of Cultural Tourist

Before discussing the definition and different approaches surrounding the concept of cultural tourism, it is necessary to briefly identify discrete types of cultural tourists. Stebbins suggests that in general, cultural tourists can be divided into two main categorize of specialized and general where both types tend to avoid commercial ventures located within their area of interest.

Categories of Cultural Tourists in General

The 'general' cultural tourist	The 'specialized' cultural tourist
Makes a hobby of visiting different geographic sites. Over time, as general cultural tourists increase their knowledge of different cultures, they may become specialized cultural tourists who focus on one or a small number of geographic sites or cultural entities.	Repeatedly visits a particular city, region, or country in search of a board cultural understanding of the place, or goes to different cities, regions, countries in search of exemplars of, for instance, a kind of art, history, festival, or museum.

However, Stebbins list for different cultural tourist is quite general and despite what its name suggests, is not specifically related to cultural tourism. A more detailed typology for cultural tourism by McKercher and Du Gros categorize cultural tourists in response to their depth of experience and also the importance of culture, as a motivator, in their travel. The first three types of cultural tourists; the purposeful, the sightseeing and the serendipitous can, arguably, are considered as the primary cultural tourist due to their main motivator and experience for choosing a destination for the sake of cultural values. Comparing to the list provided by Stebbins, these three types of cultural tourist can be regarded as specialized and the other two; casual and incidental, are within the category of general cultural tourists.

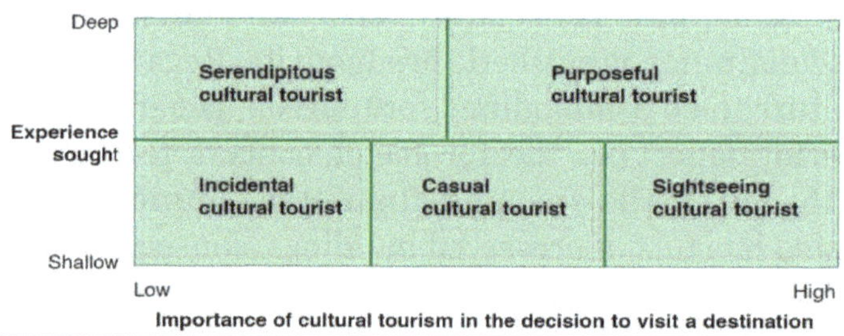

- **The purposeful cultural tourist**
  Cultural tourism is the primary motive for visiting a destination and the tourist has a very deep cultural experience;
- **The sightseeing cultural tourist**
  Cultural tourism is a primary reason for visiting a destination, but the experience is less deep;
- **The serendipitous cultural tourist**
  A tourist who does not travel for cultural reasons, but who, after participating, ends up having a deep cultural tourism experience;
- **The casual cultural tourist**
  Cultural tourism is a weak motive for travel and the resulting experience is shallow;
- **The incidental cultural tourist**
  This tourist does not travel for cultural reasons, but nonetheless participates in some activities and has shallow experiences.

Typology of cultural tourist.

Cultural Tourism in Context

The main usage of the term cultural tourism involves the consumption of a wide range of cultural manifestations like heritage, art, folklore and etc. by tourists. Cultural tourism can be generally seen as a sociocultural relationship between people which is promoted, moderated and mediated by a range of various actors including, planners, politicians, researchers, marketing professionals, travel agencies and so on. Cultural tourism can be regarded as a meeting between social systems and cultures which will produce changes in both of them. As a social practice, cultural tourism reconstructs or constructs identities (e.g. nationalism, social identities, and transnationalism) and will eventually contribute to globalization and framing a globalized world.

Bonink identifies two approaches regarding the definition of cultural tourism; the 'sites and monuments' approach, focusing on explaining the type of attractions visited by cultural tourists, which mainly describes culture as a product. This quantitative approach simply assumes cultural tourism as a consumer of cultural attractions and proposes a relatively limited view of the motivations and activities of cultural tourists, thus restricting its analysis to specific attractions and sites. For instance, site and monument approach of cultural tourism, typically, consider the following attractions and sites as 'intangible' and 'tangible' expressions of culture which attracts cultural tourists.

- Archaeological sites and museums.
- Architecture (ruins, famous buildings, whole towns).
- Art, sculpture, crafts, galleries, festivals, events.
- Music and dance (classical, folk, contemporary).
- Drama (theatre, films, dramatists).
- Language and literature study, tours, events.
- Religious festivals, pilgrimages.
- Complete (folk or primitive) cultures and sub-cultures.

The second approach, called 'the conceptual approach', attempts to define cultural tourism in a more qualitative way through analyzing the practices, experiences and meanings of cultural tourist in contact with other places and cultures. As Richards describes; 'as with tourism in general, conceptual definitions of cultural tourism attempt to describe the motive and meanings attached to cultural tourism activity.' For example, McIntosh and Goeldner define 'cultural tourism' including 'all aspects of travel, whereby travelers become familiar with the heritage and history of others or their contemporary ways of life or thought". In other words, 'the processes and products of other cultures are what cultural tourism offer to cultural tourists.

Furthermore, Pereiro, argues that from this standpoint, cultural tourism can be defined in a different way; 'as a process of commodification, a nostalgia for heritage and the past, a psychological experience, process of learning and curiosity, a modern form of pilgrimage, as an industry which represents cultural values and as a specific way of cultural consumption'.

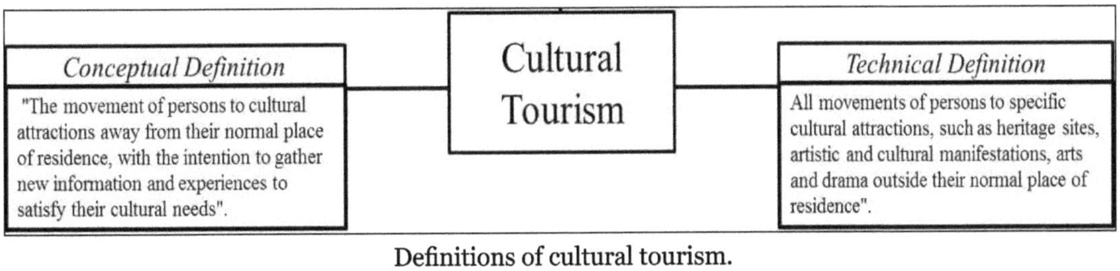

Definitions of cultural tourism.

Further study on the conceptual definition of cultural tourism suggests this approach stimulated a move away from culture as product to culture as process or 'way of life" definitions of culture which is visible in the growing interest of tourists in experiencing lifestyle, customs and everyday life of people in different destinations. In other words, the previous preoccupation of tourism with natural resources and landscapes seems to be more involved in sensory and symbolic consumption of the ideas and images associated with particular destinations. This expanding and diverse pattern of cultural consumption for tourists primarily dealing with intangible elements make defining the concept of culturally motivated and also cultural tourism even more difficult.

The Importance of Identity

One of the most important 'components' of cultural tourism and tourism in general is the issue of identity. Particularly in recent years, the struggle for creating and meditating the identity has become an inseparable feature of cultural tourism. In other words, identity is assumed as a primary value both for cultural tourists and their hosts; the hosts want to promote a unique identity for their communities to lure visitors thus bringing the associated benefits of tourism, on the other hand this unique 'local' identity will satisfy the thirst of cultural consumption and help distinguish the cultural tourist. According to Richards and Pereiro the factors responsible for emergence of identity as a key element in cultural tourism are;

- The need for regions to distinguish themselves.
- The search for new forms of community.
- The need to valorize culture.
- The shift towards experiential tourism.
- Postmodern/postcolonial reification of identity.

Identity itself can be described as a 'process of social construction of meanings that utilizes cultural attributes' which occurs in the context of power relations." In order to clearly understand the emerging role of identity in cultural tourism, it is noteworthy to briefly describe three basic types of identity distinguished by Manuel Castells.

Three Basic Types of Identity

'Legitimated' Identity	'Resistant' Identity	'Projectual' Identity
Created by dominant institutions to legitimate their power over other social actors.	A claim by social actors in low social positions who are stigmatized by the dominant groups. It is a construction of alternative social principles of organization, it is more communal and represents a defensive identity against exclusion and domination.	Where social actors manipulate their cultural materials and construct a new identity that redefines their position in society and transforms the social structure.

Cultural tourism can play an important role and contribute to all these three types of identity; for instance; promoting 'national monuments' thus supporting legitimate identity, creating 'alternative' cultural itineraries for resistant identity and of course promoting new images for communities for projectual identity. Therefore, it is obvious that cultural tourism can play a crucial role in construction and reconstruction of identity for the sake of tourism consumption. In other words, as a 'mechanism of cultural and social change', tourism has a significant influence on transformation of identity where in some situations cultural tourism may reinforce this identity, in other cases it may add new senses and meanings to peoples and spaces thus altering and transforming identity fundamentally. However, no matter how this process of 'commodification of culture' proceeds, the social costs of it cannot be ignored.

Furthermore, another factor which reveals the close relationship between identity and cultural tourism is the current issue of globalization along with loosened social ties, decline in traditional family forms and structure and individualism. This emerging situation calls for a redefined 'symbolic constructions for communities' where cultural tourism can acts as an ideological stimulus in order to promote a new image and identity in response to the contemporary social relation thus modifying the borders and boundaries between different human groups both in local and global level.,

Archaeological Tourism

Archaeological tourism refers to the process whereby people travel to historical and archeological places of interest. The reason why it is called archaeological tourism is due to the fact that it is often aimed at arranging visits to archeological sites where places and artifacts dating back to antiquity have been discovered, such as the pyramids in Egypt. Archeological tourism may be a means for the tourists to satisfy their curiosity regarding the ancient sites or it may be for the purpose of educating the tourists who may be students and scholars.

Most times, it is the government of the region where the antiquities are located to promote archaeological tourism as a means of educating people about their rich cultural heritage, or simply as a means to make some money from the tourists who visit. Tourism is such a big business that some economies are mainly dependent on it for their survival. For this reason, some governments might promote their culture and encourage archeological tourism as a means to generate more funds. Tourists spend money on airfare, transportation, food, accommodation, services and the purchase of artifacts. The government also gains from the taxes imposed on the expenditure by such tourists.

An archaeological tourism destination could be anything of interest ranging from museums where artifacts are housed to the actual excavation sites themselves. Sometimes the archeological tourism involves other related features, such as recreations of historical sites or the simulation of more modern sites to look like some culturally relevant ones that may no longer exist. For instance, the simulation could include something like a ghost town that looks like a town from antiquity would look.

One of the drawbacks of archaeological tourism is the danger that may be posed to truly historical sites by hordes of tourists who descend on these places in large numbers. Even with strict restrictions, there is always the danger of some form of damage to such places, possibly affecting the pristineness of historical sites. For example, when tourists visit caves with ancient paintings on the walls, the constant traffic of human beings may lead to an erosion of the properly preserved status of the place. It is the government of the region where the archaeological tourism is taking place that must decide if the revenue it is deriving from the tourist trade is a good compromise for the reduction in the historical value of the sites.

Holocaust Tourism

The Holocaust tourism is a term used by the media in relation to round-trip travel to destinations connected with the extermination of Jews during the Holocaust in World War II, including visits to sites of Jewish martyrology such as former Nazi death camps and concentration camps turned into state museums. It belongs to a category of the so-called 'roots tourism' usually across parts of Central Europe, or more generally, the Western-style dark tourism to sites of death and disaster.

Main track of Auschwitz-Birkenau.

It has come to symbolize the systematic extermination of approximately six million European Jews by Nazi Germany in occupied territories from 1933 to 1945. The term can also be applied to mean the estimated five to seven million non-Jewish victims who were murdered by the Nazis in the same time period.

Dark Tourism Spectrum

The term 'dark tourism' was first coined in 1996. According to P. R. Stone, there is a *dark tourism spectrum*, which differentiates between the shades of the dark tourism:

darkest	darker	dark	light	lighter	lightest

The spectrum aids in identifying the intensity of both the framework of supply and the consumption. The darkest tourism is characterized by the following elements: education orientation, historic background, location authenticity in terms of relics (non-purposefulness), and limited tourism infrastructure. The objects of lightest tourism have mostly opposite features: entertainment orientation, commercial centralization, inauthenticity, commercial purposefulness, and higher level of tourism infrastructure. Professor William F. S. Miles stipulates that death and violent events – transmitted between generations through survivors and witnesses – are darker than other events. Miles also notes that the level of darkness of a tourist destination may partially depend on the family background of the prospective tourists.

Stone distinguishes seven dark suppliers, which create the dark tourism product and experience. The model of seven dark suppliers demonstrate dark tourism as multi-faceted phenomenon, with the extermination camp at Auschwitz-Birkenau conceivably the darkest in terms of influence. The Dark Camps of Genocide are sites where genocide and violence were actually perpetrated. All such sites belong to this category. Auschwitz was the largest of the Nazi death camps in World War II, and is at the top of this list. Holocaust sites usually depend on government's sponsorship. Among the seven dark suppliers are also war sites and battlefields (Dark Conflict Sites), places of remembrances (Dark Shrines), cemeteries of famous people (Dark Resting Places), prisons and courthouses (Dark Dungeons), exhibits associated with death and suffering (Dark Exhibitions), and finally, the tourist sites which emphasize entertainment (Dark Fun Factories).

Postmemory and Jewish Identity

March of the living from Auschwitz to Birkenau.

Holocaust tourism sites are related to 'postmemory' as well as cultural identity, with postmemory being an important element in the motivations of Holocaust tourists. Marianne Hirsch defines it in the following way.

Postmemory characterizes the experience of those who grow up dominated by narratives that preceded their birth, whose own belated stories are evacuated by the stories of the previous generation shaped by traumatic events that can be neither understood nor recreated.

Postmemory is an interrelation between survivors, and post-Holocaust generations of Jews, to save and transmit the Holocaust experience. The first studies regarding the second generation began to appear in the 1970s. For example, Helen Epstein's 1979 book *Children of the Holocaust: Conversations with Sons and Daughters of Survivors* consists of interviews with survivors' children from all over the world.

Some survivors' children's identities are dependent on their parents' Holocaust experience. The Jewish visits to Holocaust sites are often efforts to explore the origins of their identity. Erica Lehrer considers this Jewish identity quest as 'a way to step into the flow of family, community, and history from which one feels displaced". Many Jewish tours are made to establish a connection of survivors and second generation with an unknown place and or identity.

In Central Europe

Holocaust map of Poland.

During the last 20 years Central Europe has become the most popular region for Jewish heritage travels. The recent increase in tourism is due to several historic events which have opened the region: Poland's Solidarity movement; Mikhail Gorbachev's policies of glasnost and perestroika; and the dissolution of the Soviet Union.

Though many of the tourists have no direct experience of the Holocaust, many Holocaust tours visit authentic Holocaust sites, such as cemeteries and crematoria. Two principal destinations of Holocaust tourism are Poland and Israel. The relationship between those two countries in Holocaust tourism was best illustrated by the anthropologist Jack Kugelmass who employed a 'performance approach' to the Shoa group missions.

The trip is orchestrated so as to minimize contact with modern Poland and instil a negative sense of place. The death camps serve as condensation symbols for the entire Jewish past. By identifying with the Shoa dead, the participants seek to reaffirm their own vulnerability as opposed to their privileged position as Jews in American society, while pledging to resist assimilation. The trips inevitably end in Israel, mythicized as 'the Jewish future.'

In Israel, the March of the Living (MOTL) was established in 1988, which organizes Holocaust tours for teenagers. Annually, MOTL sends thousands of young people from more than fifty countries to Poland and Israel. Poland is one of the countries most visited by Holocaust tourists due to the number of death camps in Poland. Prior to World War II, Poland had the largest Jewish community in Europe, of which over three million (90%) were murdered.

Death and labor camps were built in Central Europe by the German occupational authorities in the late 1930s and early 1940s, many of them in Poland, of which Auschwitz was the first and largest.

In the period between 1941 and 1944 other death camps were established by the Reich in occupied Poland including Majdanek (in Lublin); Birkenau (in Brzezinka); Treblinka (near the village of Treblinka); Bełżec (south-east of Lublin); Sobibór (near the village of Sobibor); Chełmno (near the village of Chełmno nad Nerem).

Critical View

Holocaust tourism, despite its short existence, has come under criticism. Polish journalist and Jewish activist Konstanty Gebert noted:

"People tend to forget that the important thing about Polish Jews is not that they waited 900 years for the Germans to come and kill them, but that they actually did something for those 900 years".

—Konstanty Gebert, Living in the Land of Ashes

Anthropologist Jack Kugelmass wrote that the American trips to Poland, sponsored by the Israeli Ministry of Education, promote death rather than life, because the Holocaust sites allow for a strong emotional appeal to a mythologised identity. By the same token, the propagandist messages imposed by the organizers upon students participating in the Shoah voyages are nationalistic rather than universalistic, and inevitably, impact on their empathy toward the Palestinians as well. The criticism of the Shoah group missions by the *Israeli News and Opinion* had focused on its economic aspect, with individual members calling for a generalized boycott of Poland's Holocaust-related sites. In order to stop the infusion of tourism monies, prominent Rabbis advocated that Jews refrain from going to Poland even if they wished to participate only in the official March of the Living.

'These types of [forum] posts indicate that many Jews are willing to sacrifice the benefits of touring historic sites in order to restore lost equity and potentially retaliate against entire nations and their citizens, sixty years after a particular event Further, these attempts were often found to be undertaken by people who were not directly involved in the inequitable event, but who experienced the effects of victimization indirectly".

—J. S. Podoshen, J. M. Hunt

Quest Tourism Alternative

Quest tourism, or the 'roots tourism', is a type of cultural and ethnographic tourism focused on Jewish heritage and their extermination as a historical tragedy. This term was first used by E. Lehrer. It is different from Holocaust tourism because of its orientation to the tragic aspect of Jewish Heritage. Quest tourists have specific motivations and may be characterized by the following features:

- They are, as a rule, descendants of Holocaust survivors;
- They travel individually or with close friends and family;
- They are highly interested in travel;
- They possess strong postmemory;
- Their goal is to reveal the story and overcome the communal ideology.

Virtual Jewish Communities

There are three communities on the internet in which Jewish-related concerns and news are disseminated, particularly regarding Holocaust tourism in Germany and across Central Europe. As described by J. S. Podoshen and J. M. Hunt they are:

- Jewish Current Events. A primarily North American and Israeli forum with thousands of postings concerning world events, as well as Jewish-related news from global Jewish periodicals.
- Religious Judaism. A community of over four thousands American orthodox and conservative Jews, whose main interest is Judaism and its spread throughout the world. The community is subdivided into groups based on geographic areas. The group has published over one million posts, and according to the community's archive, the Holocaust in relation to tourism is one of the most discussed topics.
- Israeli News and Opinion. A site made up of Jews living in and near Israel, which discusses news from popular Israeli and Jewish press sources.

Dracula Tourism

Dracula tourism is a type of cultural tourism involving travel to sites associated with Dracula and his real or imaginary travels. There is Dracula Tourism in Transylvania, Romania and in the United Kingdom.

Bran Castle.

The most well-known Dracula Tourism locations to visit in Romania are: Dracula Museum in Bucharest, that presents both the story of real-life Dracula, the Wallachian prince Vlad III Dracula, aka the Impaler and also the one of the mythical Dracula, the blood-thirsty vampire.

Bran Castle ('Castelul Bran"), considered to be the home of Dracula.

- The City of Sighisoara, where you can visit the house in which Vlad the Impaler was born.

Old Princely Court ('Palatul Curtea Veche") in Bucharest.

Snagov Monastery ('Manastirea Snagov"), where, according to the legend, Vlad's remains were buried.

- The ruins of the Poenari Fortress (considered to be the authentic Dracula's Castle).
- The village of Arefu, where Dracula legends are still told.
- The city of Brasov, where Vlad led raids against the Saxons merchants.

Although Dracula tourism is a popular attraction in Romania, government leaders prefer other attractions within the country to be Romania's image. The National Tourism Masterplan restricted any Dracula theme parks from 2007 to 2026 to be initiated. The Romanian government views Dracula tourism as a false image of Romania, as Dracula was from a fictional novel rather than a piece of Romanian history. Despite this, Dracula tourism has made an impact on the country's economy in the past and currently there are multiple attractions within the country.

Initially Romania's government did not view Dracula tourism as problematic due to the positive economic change. Romania's historical Vlad the Impaler was the focus of the tours.

Dracula Park

Dracula Park was a theme park proposition by Radu Florescu in 1995. The idea was to attract tourists worldwide and bring a larger audience to Romania and its identity with the fictional Transylvanian vampire.

There were over 5,000 share holders and multiple attractions were planned for the park, including a hotel.

The theme park idea was rejected until 2001, six years after the initial proposal.

Dracula Park gained widespread attention in its development. There was controversy on the theme park and if it would be harmful to Romania's image, and the Dracula Park project was dropped.

Heritage Tourism

Cultural heritage tourism (or just heritage tourism or diaspora tourism) is a branch of tourism oriented towards the cultural heritage of the location where tourism is occurring.

Tatev.

Beiteddine Palace.

Wudang Mountains.

Giza.

The National Trust for Historic Preservation in the United States defines heritage tourism as 'traveling to experience the places, artifacts and activities that authentically represent the stories and people of the past", and 'heritage tourism can include cultural, historic and natural resources".

Culture

Culture has always been a major part of travel, as the development of the Grand Tour from the 16th century onwards attests. In the 20th century, some people have claimed, culture ceased to be the objective of tourism; tourism is now culture. Cultural attractions play an important role in tourism at all levels, from the global highlights of world culture to attractions that underpin local identities.

Culture, heritage and the arts have long contributed to appeal of tourist destination. However, in recent years 'culture' has been rediscovered as an important marketing tool to attract those travellers with special interests in heritage and arts.

Cultural heritage tourism defines as cultural heritage tourism is the fastest growing segment of the tourism industry because there is a trend toward an increase specialization among tourists. This trend is evident in the rise in the volume of tourists who seek adventure, culture, history, archaeology and interaction with local people.

Cultural heritage tourism is important for various reasons; it has a positive economic and social impact, it establishes and reinforces identity, it helps preserve the cultural heritage, with culture as an instrument it facilitates harmony and understanding among people, it supports culture and helps renew tourism. As Benjamin Porter and Noel B. Salazar have ethnographically documented, however, cultural heritage tourism can also create tensions and even conflict between the different stakeholders involved.

Cultural heritage tourism has a number of objectives that must be met within the context of sustainable development such as; the conservation of cultural resources, accurate interpretation of resources, authentic visitors experience, and the stimulation of the earned revenues of cultural resources. We can see, therefore, that cultural heritage tourism is not only concerned with identification, management and protection of the heritage values but it must also be involved in understanding the impact of tourism on communities and regions, achieving economic and social benefits, providing financial resources for protection, as well as marketing and promotion.

Heritage tourism involves visiting historical or industrial sites that may include old canals, railways, battlegrounds, military sites, etc. The overall purpose is to gain an appreciation of the past. It also refers to the marketing of a location to members of a diaspora who have distant family roots there.

Immigration

Decolonization and immigration form the major background of much contemporary heritage tourism. Falling travel costs have also made heritage tourism possible for more people.

Another possible form involves religious travel or pilgrimages. Many Catholics from around the world come to the Vatican and other sites such as Lourdes or Fátima. Islam commands its followers to take the *hajj* to Mecca, thus differentiating it somewhat from tourism in the usual sense, though the trip can also be a culturally important event for the pilgrim.

Heritage tourism can also be attributed to historical events that have been dramatised to make them more entertaining. For example, a historical tour of a town or city using a theme such as ghosts or Vikings. Heritage tourism focuses on certain historical events, rather than presenting a balanced view of that historical period. Its aim may not always be the presentation of accurate historical facts, as opposed to economically developing the site and surrounding area. As a result, heritage tourism can be seen as a blend of education, entertainment, preservation and profit.

Indigenous Peoples

Anthropology and Ethnology were two major disciplines interested by the life of aborigines, their customs and political structures. Although, the firsts fieldworkers were not interested in expanding the colonization of main European powers, the fact was that their notes, books and field-work notes were employed by colonial officials to understand the aboriginal mind. From that moment on, anthropology developed a strange fascination for the Other's culture. The concepts of heritage and colonization were inextricably intertwined.

Another problem with heritage tourism is the effect on indigenous peoples whose land and culture is being visited by tourists. If the indigenous people are not a part of the majority, or ruling power in the country, they may not benefit from the tourism as greatly as they should. For example, in Mexico tourism has increased because of the predicted end of the Maya Calendar. However, the indigenous Maya are not benefitting from the increased traffic through the ruins and other cultural landmarks.

Promotion and Facilitation

Heritage tourism is supported by municipalities through promotion and tourist information in many countries and their administrative units, e.g. cities as Polish Bydgoszcz or Warsaw.

There are also many forms of presenting selected tourist topics in a harmonized way, for instance European Route of Brick Gothic and many others (Cultural Route of the Council of Europe).

Music Tourism

Music tourism is the act of visiting a city or town, to see a music festival or other music performances. This sort of tourism is particularly important to small villages such as Glastonbury, as well as large cities like Glasgow.

The fairly recent jam band phenomenon is a contemporary example that encourages music tourism. Music festivals are visited by many tourists annually.

The Artful Music Tourist Board is a movement, started to celebrate this, in 2003 by musicians and their friends at The Paradise Bar (now Royal Albert pub) in London, UK.

Music-related Events and Destinations

There are a large number of music festivals held around the world, usually annually, that attract non-local visitors. The self-proclaimed largest music festival in the world is Summerfest, an 11-day event in Milwaukee, Wisconsin with an annual attendance of nearly 1,000,000 people.

There are also a number of annual carnivals, events that include music, dancing and street parties. Some major ones include Rio Carnival in Brazil, which attracts 500,000 foreign visitors annually, and the Salvador de Bahia carnival, which is the largest street party, and attracts crowds of up to two million people throughout its week-long duration.

The Notting Hill Carnival (London, UK) is one of the largest street parties in Europe and attracts around one million people each year.

The Love Parade, an electronic dance music festival in Germany held from 1989 to 2010, saw crowds of 1.6 million at its peak.

There are hundreds of annual jazz festivals around the world, with the largest, the Montreal International Jazz Festival, seeing 2.5 million attendees every year, one third of whom are tourists.

Overall, an estimated 10 million people travel internationally each year for the main purpose of watching or participating in a music or cultural festival.

There are also some cities and areas that serve as year-round destinations for music-related travel, such as New Orleans for Dixieland, zydeco and other music, some cities in Europe (including Bayreuth in Germany, Vienna in Austria. Aix-en-Provence in France, La Scala in Milan) for opera and classical music, and Britain for rock music.

Pop-culture Tourism

Pop-culture tourism is the act of traveling to locations featured in popular literature, film, music, or any other form of media. Also referred to as a "Location Vacation".

Field of Dreams.

Pop-culture tourism is in some respects akin to pilgrimage, with its modern equivalents of places of pilgrimage, such as Elvis Presley's Graceland and the grave of Jim Morrison in Père Lachaise Cemetery.

Locations

Popular destinations have included:

Comics

- Metropolis, Illinois, declared by DC Comics to be the home of *Superman*.

Films

- Los Angeles, California area film studios.

- New York City, New York urban area featured in hundreds of Hollywood and American films.
- Salzburg, Austria, where many scenes from *The Sound of Music* were filmed.
- Tunisia, location of the filming of the *Star Wars* films, began in 1977.
- The Field of Dreams, a baseball field featured in the 1989 film of the same name.
- Petra, Jordan, where visits went from the thousands to the millions after the climactic scene of the 1989 film *Indiana Jones and the Last Crusade* was filmed in Al Khazneh.
- Wallace Monument, Stirling, dedicated to Scottish hero William Wallace. Saw a visitor rise of 160,000 after the 1995 film *Braveheart*.
- Burkittsville, Maryland, where tourists re-create the most gruesome scenes from the 1999 film *The Blair Witch Project*.
- New Zealand, after *The Lord of the Rings* was filmed there.
- Alnwick Castle, location of Hogwarts in the *Harry Potter* film series.
- Santa Ynez Valley in Central California where much of the 2004 film *Sideways* took place.
- Rosslyn Chapel, Scotland and Lincoln Cathedral, England. Locations used in *The Da Vinci Code* film.
- Brevard and Transylvania County, North Carolina. Filming location of *The Hunger Games*.
- Norway, where tourism increased after the 2013 Disney film Frozen was released.

Folklores

- Loch Ness in the Scottish highlands, home of the mythical Loch Ness Monster.
- Sherwood Forest, Nottinghamshire, England, associated with Robin Hood.
- Tintagel Castle in South-West England, association with King Arthur.

Literature

- Ashdown Forest, East Sussex, England, setting for Winnie-the-Pooh in the 1920s. The game Poohsticks is a popular attraction.
- Stratford-upon-Avon, Warwickshire, England, birthplace of William Shakespeare, receives about 4.9 million visitors a year from all over the world.
- Prince Edward Island, in which the 1908 Canadian novel *Anne of Green Gables* takes place, is a popular attraction for tourists, notably from Japan where the first translated edition was published in 1952.
- Forks, Washington, primary setting of the *Twilight* series of novels and films.

Music

- Abbey Road, London, known by the 1969 album *Abbey Road* by The Beatles whose cover features the Beatles walking across the zebra crossing of the road.
- Liverpool, England, for fans of The Beatles. A museum dedicated to them 'The Beatles Story' is situated at the Albert Dock. The reconstructed 'Cavern', the club they played in before becoming famous is also a stop for Beatles pilgrims. A bus tour of the city entitled The Magical Mystery Tour, visits many sites associated with the group including former homes of The Beatles.
- Graceland, Memphis, Tennessee, a mansion which was owned by Elvis Presley. It serves as his biographical museum since 1982.

Television Dramas

- Istanbul for fans of Turkish television drama.
- Pin Oak Court, Vermont South, Victoria, a suburban Melbourne shooting location for soap opera *Neighbours* from 1985.
- Tom's Restaurant which is known to many as Monk's from *Seinfeld.*
- North Bend, Washington and Twede's Cafe, the shooting location of the Double R Diner, where much of the 1990 television series *Twin Peaks* was filmed.
- Roslyn, Washington, which stood in for Cicely, Alaska in the television series *Northern Exposure.*
- Chuncheon, South Korea, where the 2002 KBS2 television drama series *Winter Sonata* took place.
- Tobermory, Isle of Mull, Scotland, Location of the popular children's programme *Balamory.*
- Albuquerque, New Mexico. The location of the AMC television series *Breaking Bad.*
- Highclere Castle, location of the 2010s drama series *Downton Abbey.*

Japanese Anime and Manga

- Enoshima (Shōnan) and Kamakura district, originally a local tourist spot near Tokyo. Many Japanese anime and manga series, such as *Ping Pong* (1996), *Squid Girl* (2007–2016), *Tsuritama* (2012), *Tari Tari* (2012), and one-off episodes in other series, took place there. Due to appearance in the opening theme of the 1990s anime series *Slam Dunk*, an ordinary level crossing of the Enoshima Electric Railway, near Kamakurakōkōmae Station, became popular attraction for tourists, notably from China and Taiwan.

Intentional Pop-culture Tourism Attractions

- Vulcan, Alberta, Canada. In the early 1990s this small rural community began to explore ways it could capitalize on the coincidence of the Town's name being the same as popular Star Trek Character, Mr. Spock's home planet: *Vulcan*, to develop its local tourism industry.

Literary Tourism

Literary tourism is a type of cultural tourism that deals with places and events from fictional texts as well as the lives of their authors. This could include following the route taken by a fictional character, visiting particular place associated with a novel or a novelist, such as their home, or visiting a poet's grave. Some scholars regard literary tourism as a contemporary type of secular pilgrimage. There are also long-distance walking routes associated with writers, such as the Thomas Hardy Way.

Literary tourists are specifically interested in how places have influenced writing and at the same time how writing has created place. In order to become a literary tourist you need only book-love and an inquisitive mindset; however, there are literary guides, literary maps, and literary tours to help you on your way. There are also many museums associated with writers, and these are usually housed in buildings associated with a writer's birth or literary career, such as their home.

John Shakespeare's house, believed to be Shakespeare's birthplace.

While most literary tourism is focused on famous works, more modern works that are written to specifically promote tourism are called tourism fiction. Modern tourism fiction can include travel guides within the story showing readers how to visit the real places in the fictional tales. With recent technological advances in publishing, digital tourism fiction books can even allow literary tourists to follow direct links to tourism websites related to the story. This can be done on new e-reading devices like the Kindle, iPad, iPhone, smart phones, tablets, and regular desktop and laptop computers. These links within the story allow readers to instantly learn about the real places without doing their own web searches.

The first classic novel to take advantage of tourism fiction technology was F. Scott Fitzgerald's *This Side of Paradise: Interactive Tourism Edition*, published by the Southeastern Literary Tourism Initiative in 2012. The tourism edition offered web links to tours of Princeton University, where Fitzgerald attended in real life and where the fictional protagonist in the novel Amory Blaine attended. The tourism edition also offered links to Montgomery, Alabama, where Fitzgerald fell in love with his future wife Zelda Sayre, much like the fictional character Amory fell in love with Rosalind.

In addition to visiting author and book sites, literary tourists often engage in bookstore tourism, browsing local bookshops for titles specifically related to the sites as well as other regional books and authors.

Literary tourism is a National Research Foundation-funded project in KwaZulu-Natal, South Africa. The project, KZN Literary Tourism, has a Literary Map connecting authors whose lives or work is tied in some significant way to specific places in KwaZulu-Natal. Each author entry contains a short biography, a selected bibliography and an excerpt from the author's work that relates to the place identified in the map.

Bookstore Tourism

Bookstore tourism is a type of cultural tourism that promotes independent bookstores as a group travel destination. It started as a grassroots effort to support locally owned and operated bookshops, many of which have struggled to compete with large bookstore chains and online retailers.

Those who promote bookstore tourism encourage schools, libraries, reading groups and other miscellaneous organizations to create day-trips and literary outings to cities and towns with a concentration of independent bookstores. Groups of various sizes around the U.S. have offered such excursions, usually via a chartered bus, and often incorporating book signings, author home tours and historical sites. They also encourage local booksellers to attract bibliophiles to their communities by employing bookstore tourism as an economic development tool. Others benefiting include local retailers, restaurants, bus companies and travel professionals. The effort also provides organizations with an outreach opportunity to support reading and literacy.

The bookselling, publishing, and motorcoach industries have recognized the concept's potential as a group travel niche and marketing tool.

Book Towns

A book town is a town or village with a large number of used book or antiquarian book stores. These stores, as well as literary festivals, attract bibliophile tourists. A number of the book towns are members of the International Organisation of Book Towns.

When trade in used books has now become a real growth industry, it has several reasons:

It has never been written so many new books annually, and in the ordinary bookstore, the books have to turn away quickly for the new books of the year. We buy more books than before, but changing life situations, more often changing workplaces and living conditions make it difficult for many to get rid of some of the books they've collected.

We have more free time and can now read many of the books we did not have time to read before – but which can now only be purchased from those who sell used books.

The world's first book village is isolated in Wales. Richard Booth opened an antiquarian bookshop in the village of Hay-on-Wye in 1961, with the contents of a container of books brought from New York. Today, the place, which does not even have 2,000 inhabitants, has over 25 antique shops. Many of them specialize in individual topics. The place attracts many tourists. The tourism is further promoted through book events.

Following the concept of Hay, further book villages in Europe and occasionally on other continents have emerged. The book villages organize themselves in the IOB, the International Organization of Booktowns.

The first book village in Germany and the German speaking area was founded in September 1997. Mühlbeck and the neighboring village of Friedersdorf in the district of Anhalt-Bitterfeld now have about 9 bookshops with fewer than 3000 inhabitants. The foundation stone was 70,000 books collected throughout Germany. Today, around one million books are on offer.

Book Trips

In North America, special trips have been organized since 2003 to visit independent bookshops. Also signing sessions, houses of authors and literary-historical places can be destination. Schools, libraries and others are encouraged to organize day trips.

References

- What-is-archaeological-tourism: wisegeek.com, Retrieved 18 March, 2019
- Hovi, Tuomas (2014). "The Use of History in Dracula Tourism in Romania" (PDF). Folklore: Electronic Journal of Folklore. 57: 55–78. doi:10.7592/FEJF2014.57.hovi
- Porter, Benjamin W. and Noel B. Salazar (2005). "Heritage tourism, conflict, and the public interest". International Journal of Heritage Studies. 11 (5): 361–370. doi:10.1080/13527250500337397
- Comer, Douglas (2011). Tourism and Archaeological Heritage Management at Petra: Driver to Development Or Destruction?. Springer. pp. 5–6. ISBN 9781461414803. Retrieved July 17, 2014
- Bookstore-tourism-39030: hisour.com, Retrieved 25 July, 2019

4
Medical Tourism

People traveling abroad in order to get medical treatment, is called medical tourism. It generally takes from less-developed countries, not having enough medical facilities, to developed countries. Wellness tourism, fertility tourism and dental tourism are some examples of it. All these diverse medical tourisms have been carefully analyzed in this chapter.

Medical tourism can be defined as the process of traveling outside the country of residence for the purpose of receiving medical care. Growth in the popularity of medical tourism has captured the attention of policy-makers, researchers and the media. Originally, the term referred to the travel of patients from less-developed countries to developed nations in pursuit of the treatments not available in their homeland.

Today we are experiencing both qualitative and quantitative shifts in patient mobility, as people travel from richer to less-developed countries in order to access health services. Such shift is mostly driven by the relative low-cost of treatments in less developed nations, the availability of inexpensive flights and increased marketing and online consumer information about the availability of medical services.

What really puts the word "tourism" in medical tourism concept is that people often stay in the foreign country after the medical procedure. Travelers can thus take advantage of their visit by sightseeing, taking day trips or participating in any other traditional tourism activities.

Cost

Medical tourism represents a worldwide, multibillion-dollar phenomenon that is expected to grow considerably in the next decade. For the individual interested in health services, cost is the key factor involved in the decision to receive medical care abroad.

As healthcare costs in the US and other parts of the world are excessively soaring, many employers and insurance companies started to view medical tourism as a way to lower them. More and more countries around the globe start to see the financial benefits from this emerging market, so they offer premium medical services at notably lower prices.

The primary reason that clinics and hospitals in the developing countries are able to lower their prices is directly related to the nation's economic status. The direct correlation with per capita gross domestic product of the country is observed, which is a proxy for income levels. As a consequence, surgery prices are from 30% to 70% lower in the countries that are promoting medical tourism when compared to the US.

Quality

There are two major components of the service quality in the health care sector - technical or mechanical quality and serviceable or functional quality. Technical equipment is at the core of the patients' diagnostic algorithm, while the functional quality is measured by the service offered in the healthcare centers (such as the services of staffs, nurses and, most importantly, the doctors towards the patient and their assistants). The service quality in medical tourism industry is a vital part in attracting customers.

One of the fundamental barriers in accepting medical tourism is the perception of inadequate quality. A key to overcome it is using adequate marketing strategies and quality assessment via accreditation from an internationally recognized institution. Such accreditation is pivotal for strengthening confidence in the quality of healthcare.

This confidence can be even stronger if accreditation is followed by an affiliation with reputable hospitals or health care systems in industrialized countries. Once healthcare providers are accredited and become a part of international referral networks, they can be appropriately rated for risks.

Treatment Types

Categories of different treatments and their availability also represent an important factor in decision to engage in medical tourism. The most common types of procedures that patients pursue during medical tourism trips are elective cosmetic surgery, dentistry, organ transplantation, cardiac surgery and orthopedic surgery.

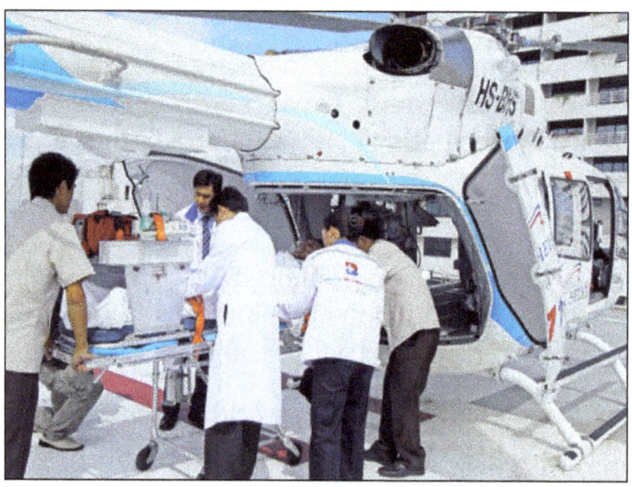

However, a wide variety of services can be obtained through medical tourism, ranging from various essential treatments to different kinds of traditional and alternative treatments. Reproductive tourism and reproductive outsourcing are growing in popularity, which is the practice of traveling abroad to engage in surrogate pregnancy, in vitrofertilization and other assisted reproductive technology methods.

In addition to cost, other major factor responsible for the increase of medical tourism is access. The lack of it, either due to the unavailability of the technology or the prohibition in the home country, can subsequently lead to medical tourism. The common examples are cytoplasmic transfer or stem cell therapy.

Wellness Tourism

Wellness tourism is travel for the purpose of promoting health and well-being through physical, psychological, or spiritual activities. While wellness tourism is often correlated with medical tourism because health interests motivate the traveler, wellness tourists are proactive in seeking to improve or maintain health and quality of life, often focusing on prevention, while medical tourists generally travel reactively to receive treatment for a diagnosed disease or condition.

Kołobrzeg, Polish resort on the coast of the Baltic Sea.

Market

Within the US $3.4 trillion spa and wellness economy, wellness tourism is estimated to total US$494 billion or 14.6 percent of all 2013 domestic and international tourism expenditures. Driven by growth in Asia, the Middle East/North Africa, Sub-Saharan Africa and developing countries, wellness tourism is expected to grow 50 percent faster than the overall tourism industry over the next five years. Market is expected to grow through 2014.

Wellness tourists are generally high-yield tourists, spending, on average, 130 percent more than the average tourist. In 2013, International wellness tourists spend approximately 59 percent more per trip than the average international tourist; domestic wellness tourists spend about 159 percent more than the average domestic tourist. Domestic wellness tourism is significantly larger than its international equivalent, representing 84 percent of wellness travel and 68 percent of expenditures (or $299 billion). International wellness tourism represents 16 percent of wellness travel and 32 percent of expenditures ($139 billion market).

The wellness tourism market includes primary and secondary wellness tourists. Primary wellness tourists travel entirely for wellness purposes while secondary wellness tourists engage in wellness-related activities as part of a trip. Secondary wellness tourists constitute the significant majority (87 percent) of total wellness tourism trips and expenditures (85 percent).

Types

Wellness travelers pursue diverse services, including physical fitness and sports; beauty treatments; healthy diet and weight management; relaxation and stress relief; meditation; yoga; and health-related education. Wellness travelers may seek procedures or treatments using conventional, alternative, complementary, herbal, or homeopathic medicine.

Hotels and Hospitality

Almost 17 million (40 percent) of US hotel guests seek to maintain a healthy lifestyle while traveling. Global hotel groups, including Intercontinental Hotels Group (IHG), Kimpton Hotels, MGM Grand Hotel, Trump Wellness Hotels, and Westin, have developed and promoted programs to attract these health-conscious guests. Programs include healthy menu options, relaxation programs, spa services, and fitness facilities and classes. As of 2012, over 80 percent of US hotels and over 90 percent of upscale US hotels offered fitness facilities. Internationally, 45 percent of hotel guests indicated that the existence of a hotel spa was an important factor in their booking decision.

Hospitals and Medical Centers

Hospitals are a significant provider of destination wellness programs. Typical programs emphasize lifestyle improvement, prevention, or health screening. Hospital and hotel partnerships often support these programs.

Resorts and Retreats

Wellness resorts and retreats offer short-term, residential programs to address specific health concerns, reduce stress, or support lifestyle improvement.

Individual Practitioners

Making up a subset of the retreat and resort offerings, individual teachers, trainers or wellness-related practitioners will privately rent resort centers, small hotels or sections of larger hotels. These retreats are themed and designed for the specific participants.

Festivals and Conferences

High profile weekends in destination locations that draw industry leaders together to deliver cutting edge, eclectic, instructive, adventurous and otherwise nourishing, healthy weekends.

Cruise and Spas

As health and wellness is becoming a growing reason for people to travel across the globe, cruise ships are increasingly gaining popularity. Spas on cruise ships can help make the voyage more relaxing and pleasurable. Numerous cruise ships are available today that provide spa and wellness treatments on board.

Destinations

Wellness tourism is now an identifiable niche market in at least 30 countries. Twenty countries accounted for 85 percent of global wellness tourism expenditures in 2012. The top five countries alone (United States, Germany, Japan, France, Austria) account for more than half the market (59 percent of expenditures).

As of 2014, the US is the largest wellness tourism market, with $180.7 billion in annual, combined international and domestic expenditures. The US is the top destination for inbound international wellness tourism, with 7.1 million international, inbound trips. Europe and high-income Asian countries are primary sources of wellness tourists traveling to the US.

Domestic tourism accounts for the majority (94 percent) of wellness trips in North America. Americans and Canadians receive — and take — few vacation days compared to workers in other countries making domestic, weekend trips the most popular wellness travel option.

Europe is the second largest wellness tourism market, with $158.4 billion in annual, combined international and domestic expenditures; the region ranks highest in number of wellness trips with 216.2 million, compared to North America's 171.7 in 2013. Europeans have long believed in health benefits derived from mineral baths, saunas, thalassotherapy, and other natural and water-based treatments. Thermal resorts and hotels in Turkey and Hungary cater to wellness tourists, many of whom are subsidized by host countries such as Norway and Denmark seeking to mitigate costs of medical procedures for patients with chronic conditions requiring expensive surgeries.

The Asia-Pacific region ranks as the third largest with $6.4 billion in annual, combined international and domestic expenditures. Wellness traditions date back thousands of years in this region, and some of those wellness practices (e.g., Ayurveda, traditional Chinese medicine (TCM), yoga, hilot, Thai massage) incorporate preventive, curative, and therapeutic aspects that lie in the cross-over area between wellness and medical tourism.

Latin America-Caribbean is the fourth largest region for wellness tourism in terms of number of trips and expenditures. Domestic tourism accounts for about 71 percent of wellness tourism trips, and 54 percent of wellness tourism expenditures.

The Middle East and Africa are currently the smallest regions for wellness tourism, where international tourists account for the majority of wellness trips and wellness expenditures. The Middle East has a long tradition of bathing associated with Turkish baths, and some older facilities are being modernized to serve spa-bound tourists. Tourism in general is on the rise in the region, and governments and private developers have been investing heavily in facilities and amenities, especially those oriented to the wealthy traveler.

In Africa, wellness tourism is concentrated in a few regions and is dominated by international tourists. South Africa reports significant domestic wellness tourism. Tunisia and Morocco have a well-developed resort spa sector primarily serving leisure vacationers from Europe.

Criticism

Wellness tourism advocates suggest that vacations improve physical well-being, happiness, and productivity, citing that health-oriented trips give travelers a fresh perspective and positively affect creativity, resilience, problem solving, and capacity for coping with stress. Yet the health benefits of wellness vacations expected and reported by vacationers have proved difficult to quantify.

Fertility Tourism

Fertility tourism or reproductive tourism is the practice of traveling to another country or jurisdiction for fertility treatment, and may be regarded as a form of medical tourism. The main reasons for fertility tourism are legal prohibitions or regulation of the sought procedure in the home country, the non-availability of a procedure in the home country, as well as lower costs in the destination country. The main procedures sought are in vitro fertilization (IVF) and donor insemination, but also surrogacy.

IVF Destinations

About 20,000 to 25,000 women (often accompanied by their partners) annually seek cross-border assisted reproductive technology (ART) services.

Destinations

Israel is the leading fertility tourism destination for in vitro fertilization (IVF) treatment. The United States is the destination of many Europeans because of the higher success rates and liberal regulations. In turn, India and other Asian countries are the main destinations for U.S. women seeking fertility treatment, being the destinations for 40% of U.S. women seeking IVF and 52%

seeking IVF with egg donation. Many travel from countries like Germany and Italy, which are very restrictive of the number of eggs that may be fertilized and how many embryos can be used for implantation or cryopreservation. In recent years, Mexico has become a popular destination for cross-border IVF treatment due to its liberal ART and egg donation policies. Even small countries such as Barbados provide JCI-accredited IVF treatment aimed at women from abroad.

Cost Factors

Women from countries such as the United States and the United Kingdom may travel for IVF treatment and medications to save money. The cost of one IVF cycle in the United States averages US$15,000, while for comparable treatment in Mexico it is about US$7,800, Thailand $6,500, and India $3,300.

Egg Donation

Egg donation is illegal in a number of European countries including Germany, Austria and Italy. Many women then will seek treatment in places where the procedure is allowed such as Spain and the United States where donors can be paid for their donation. Almost half of all IVF treatments with donor eggs in Europe are performed in Spain. IVF with anonymous egg donation is also the main ART sought by Canadians traveling to the U.S., and is the sought procedure for 80% of cross-border treatments by Canadians.

Sex Selection

Sex selection is prohibited in many countries, including the United Kingdom, Australia and Canada, India, except when it is used to screen for genetic diseases. Some women wishing to be sure of a child's sex may travel to countries where it is legal to perform a preimplantation genetic diagnosis (PGD, a potential expansion of IVF), which can be used for sex selection, such as the United States.

Risks

Many countries have no restriction on how many embryos may be transferred into the uterus at the same time, increasing the risk of multiple pregnancy and resultant potential complications. The burden of multiple births generated by placing too many embryos is carried by the patients and the home country.

Donor Insemination

A woman may go to another country to obtain artificial insemination by donor. The practice is influenced by the attitudes and sperm donation laws in the host country.

There is generally a demand for sperm donors who have no genetic problems in their family, 20/20 eyesight, with excellent visual acuity, a college degree, and sometimes a value on a certain height, age, eye colour, hair texture, blood type and ethnicity. Anecdotal evidence suggests that the inventory of taller men who are blonde and blue eyed is most popular.

Destinations

Denmark has a well-developed system of sperm export. This success mainly comes from the reputation of Danish sperm donors for being of high quality and, in contrast with the law in the other Nordic countries, gives donors the choice of being either anonymous or non-anonymous to the receiving couple. Furthermore, Nordic sperm donors tend to be tall, with rarer features like blond hair or different color eyes and a light complexion, and highly educated and have altruistic motives for their donations, partly due to the relatively low monetary compensation in Nordic countries. More than 50 countries worldwide are importers of Danish sperm, including Paraguay, Canada, Kenya, and Hong Kong. Another emerging destination for fertility tourism is Barbados. More and more Caribbean couples and couples of African origin are in need medical help to conceive, and often want eggs and sperm that match their genetic composition. For a long time, their only option was the United States; however, for over 11 years Barbados has been providing couples with the latest in cutting edge technology and has introduced new techniques.

Origins

Some countries such as United Kingdom and Sweden, have a shortage of sperm donors. Sweden now has an 18-month-long waiting list for donor sperm.

As a consequence of the shortage of donor sperm in UK in the late 1990s and the early years of the 21st century, British women travelled to Belgium and Spain for donor insemination, until those two countries changed their laws and imposed a maximum number of children one donor may produce. Prior to the change in the law, the limit in the number of children born to each donor depended upon practitioners at fertility clinics, and Belgian and Spanish clinics were purchasing donor sperm from abroad to satisfy demand for treatments. Anonymous donation was permitted in Belgium and is a legal requirement in Spain. These two countries also allowed single heterosexual and single and coupled lesbians to undergo fertility treatment. Ironically, at the time, many Belgian and Spanish clinics were buying sperm from British clinics donated by British donors, and they were able to use that sperm according to local laws and limits. In addition, lesbian women from France and eastern Europe travelled to these countries in order to achieve a pregnancy by an anonymous donor since this treatment was not available to them in their own countries. British fertility tourists must therefore now travel to other countries particularly those that do not include children born to foreigners in their national totals of children produced by each donor. Britain also imports donor sperm from Scandinavia but can only limit the use of that donor's sperm to ten families in the UK itself, so that more children may be produced elsewhere from the same donor.

At least 250 Swedish sperm recipients travel to Denmark annually for insemination. Some of this is also due to that Denmark also allows single women to be inseminated.

It is illegal to pay donors for eggs or sperm in Canada. Women can still import commercial U.S. sperm, but that's not true for eggs, resulting in many Canadian women leaving the country for such procedures.

Dental Tourism

Dental tourism is driven by numerous factors. These factors include the high cost of local care, deferments in obtaining access to local dentists, proficient care at many international clinics, budget air travel, and the internet's capability to link 'customers' to 'brokers' of healthrelated services.

Though dental tourism will benefit some patients, increased patient movement comes with numerous risks. Lack of access to inexpensive and timely local care plays important role in prompting patients to cross the country borders and receive dental care outside their nations.

Dental tourism (also called dental vacations) is a subset of the sector known as medical tourism. It involves individuals seeking dental care outside of their local healthcare systems and may be accompanied by a vacation. Dental tourism is defined as traveling abroad for affordable dental care, dental treatment, dental surgery or dental procedures, which are generally expensive in one's own country. Increasing numbers of patients are crossing national borders and obtaining dental care at low cost clinics. Journalists commonly characterize the phenomenon of cross-border care as 'dental tourism'.

Today top class medical, dental treatment is just a flight away and it's no Secret that thousands of people from US Europe, United Kingdom and other countries travel to India for their dental treatment. India has seen a great increase in the dental tourist in recent years. The dental tourism in India has an edge over others for its cost-effective, quality and timely done dental care.

Need for Dental Tourism

If your employer provides you with dental insurance benefits you are among the fortunate few. A lot of people do not have dental insurance. So when there is a need to visit the dentist, they find themselves digging deep into their pockets. This is what has given birth to dental tourism. To such people dental tourism offers a low cost high quality alternative.

In the US, the main reason for going abroad for dental care is the cost advantage that the foreign country offers. And in some other cases, it's the difficulty in getting the urgently required care on time that leads people to find the care elsewhere. In Canada and certain European countries with national healthcare system, it's the extensive wait-lists that result into their citizens finding other sources to meet their dental care needs.

Internet plays a powerful role in connecting 'customers' to sellers of dental services. Dental clinics around the world use the internet to advertise procedures to international patients. Dental tourism companies, mainstream travel agencies selling healthrelated travel packages, and medical tourism companies likewise use the Internet to advertise 'all inclusive deals'.

These packages include dental procedures with pre-established prices, hotel rooms, air fare, ground transportation, 'VIP treatment', restaurant reservations, and side trips to popular tourist destinations.

Benefits of Dental Tourism

Low Cost

Undoubtedly, the biggest benefit of dental tourism is cost savings. Some countries are able to provide top quality dental care at a low cost because of low labor and administrative costs in those countries.

High Quality

They provide the treatment with state-of-the-art technology and modern equipment. The staff dentists are educated and well trained.

Immediate Service

The dentists work with your schedule and time frame to ensure quick access to care.

Travel Opportunities

While the primary motivation for most customers is affordable dental care, for some people it's a great opportunity to combine dental care with traveling/ vacation. Given the low cost of road, rail and air travel, you can even bring your friends or family along. Also, dental appointments don't take much time so lodging expenses are also low.

When and for which Dental Treatments/Procedures should Dental Tourism be Considered?

Dental tourism is not always a good option. Along with the cost savings on the treatment, you should also consider the time required as well as the number of visits needed for your specific case.

Sometimes, travel costs may outweigh the potential savings in which case it makes dental tourism not worthwhile. If you need braces, for example, which require frequent adjustment by your orthodontist; it may be a better idea to seek help at home unless you travel every month to the country on any other personal business trips.

The dental tourism destination you choose can also be a major factor in how much you are able to save. Again you wouldn not normally want to pack your bags and head down to other countries for your half yearly dental cleaning costing less than a thousand rupees at home.

Dental Tourism Destinations

One other important consideration is location. There are many dental tourism destinations globally that provide low cost high quality dental tourism. If you come all the way to India or go to Singapore or Argentina for a dental procedure, and something goes wrong, it is a long way to go to have to return and get them to fix it. Americans choose to go somewhere easily accessible from the US, such as San Salvador or Tijuana. In case of patients from Europe, dental tourism to Turkey and dental tourism to Hungary are common. For major dental surgeries, dental tourism to India, dental tourism to Thailand and dental tourism to Singapore are more common given the reputation for top class technology in those countries.

Despite the long travel time involved, India is a popular destination for dental tourists. It arguably has the lowest cost and highest quality of all medical and dental tourism destinations and English is widely spoken.

According to research reports on Indian Healthcare sector, the medical tourism market including dental treatments is valued to be worth over $310 million with foreign patients coming by 100,000 every year, and the market is predicted to grow to $2 billion by end of 2012.

Dental tourists choose India as their favorable destination because of the key opportunities in Indian healthcare sector in the form of efficient infrastructures and technology. The health insurance market and National medical systems here are well developed, which is convenient for visitors from the West and the Middle East. Several hospitals are accredited by the Joint Commission International (JCI) and staffed by highly trained physicians.

Expenses can be obtained in advance and many hospitals bundle services into a package deal that includes the medical procedure and the cost of treating any complications. Hotel accommodations are extra, but hospitals often have hotel rooms or can offer discounts for hotels nearby.

The important drawback of choosing long destinations is that, some major procedures often require multiple steps, or subsequent checkups, the patient may have to return to the same doctor for those reasons. Or, in the case of dental implants, if the implant is placed in another country but is restored by another doctor locally, the information about the implant can be difficult to retrieve from the original doctor. Typically though, a patient takes two trips to have implants. The first to set the base and a temporary, the second trip 4-6 months later after ones mouth has healed and accepted the implant-one has the temp removed and the permanent crown set. Two weekly trips are necessary.

One-Day-Implants are not recommended for dental tourists due to the higher failure rate of the system.

In conclusion, it can be said that with growing needs of healthcare and rising costs worldwide, one needs to find out a cost effective and non-quality compromising solution to the same.

In India, the dental tourism industry is still fledgling and is exploring its embryonic growth phases. Every industry comes with its own pros and cons. Not all dental care could be sought while travelling from one country to another. Affordable cost is an added advantage. It is expected that in years to come, with India emerging as a preferred destination for dental treatment, dental tourism in the country is expected to have a dramatic growth and this would be backed up by investments in healthcare.

References

- What-is-Medical-Tourism, health: news-medical.net, Retrieved 23 May, 2019
- Woodman, Josef (2015-02-17). Patients Beyond Borders: Everybody's Guide to Affordable, World-Class Medical Travel. ISBN 978-0990315407
- Hughes EG, Dejean D (June 2010). "Cross-border fertility services in North America: a survey of Canadian and American providers". Fertility and Sterility. 94 (1): e16–9. doi:10.1016/j.fertnstert.2009.12.008. PMID 20149916
- Dental-Tourism-Global-Competition-in-Health-Care- 226018768: researchgate.net, Retrieved 04 August, 2019

5
Adventure Tourism

The type of tourism involving exploration of places or travelling to remote areas, in order to experience the thrill of surroundings, is referred to as adventure tourism. It covers hot air ballooning, zip lining, free falling, rafting, spelunking, mountaineering, etc. This chapter has been carefully written to provide an in-depth knowledge of various kinds of adventure tourism.

Adventure Tourism is a term which is not easily defined. Different people have different perceptions of what might constitute "adventure". For one person, "adventure" may be something as simple as camping outside in a tent, or walking through a wilderness area for an hour. For another, this would be considered passive tourism, whereas adventure would mean participating in dangerous and physically (also maybe emotionally) demanding and challenging activities, such as climbing a sheer rock face or white water rafting in dangerous waters.

Even for those tourists seeking challenging experiences, the degree of challenge desired may be quite different. Some will baulk at undertaking potentially dangerous activities like walking on a rope bridge across a deep ravine, and would find a trek through the jungle at ground level sufficiently challenging. Whilst some will find another's "adventure" decidedly unpleasant, disagreeable, foolishly reckless, traumatic or boring.

Therefore, the first principle of adventure tourism is catering for difference:

- Different expectations.

- Different physical abilities.
- Different likes and dislikes.
- Different psychological make-ups.

It is not a matter of making an adventure less adventurous, or more exciting, nor is it a matter of participants' 'inferior' or 'superior' physical or psychological resilience. It is simply a matter of personal difference, and preference.

Adventure Tourism Experiences

The stimulation and intensity associated with adventure contributes to removing the experience from the routine of everyday life. Exotic surroundings, new activities, experiences beyond anything one has ever experienced contributes to a sense of escapism. Adventure is a chance to escape the everyday concerns of life. Imagine being on top of Mount Everest. Would you be thinking of anything else but just being there. Enjoying the rapture of having achieved such a feat, the wondrous view and the elation of breaking your boundaries. No wonder adventure is so popular.

The term 'Adventure Tourism' can represent many kinds of experience, and an almost infinite range of tourism situations. What they all share is a participant's sense of excitement and adventure, and of entering an experience or series of experiences that will take them out of urban areas into more natural and less obviously regulated environments.

Motivating Factors For Adventure Tourism

People are motivated to undertake adventure tourism activities for different reasons. Some may enjoy the anticipation of an unknown or uncertain outcome. This could be undertaking something new and unfamiliar or the presence of a perceived danger in the activity. This element of risk involved in an activity might be relished by some and feared by others.

There needs to be a degree of challenge in an activity for it to be considered adventurous. A challenging event might have an element of danger, unknown outcomes and degree of difficulty. This will attract different participants to the activity based upon their expectations and their willingness to cope with challenges.

There also needs to be a perceived reward on completion of the activity. This is usually the sense of meeting a challenge and pushing themselves beyond their usual comfort zone. This is referred to as an intrinsic reward, as it comes from within. There may also be extrinsic awards such as a trophy. An example would be gaining a place in a white-water kayaking race.

A sense of escapism is also important for an activity to be considered adventurous. This is why most adventure tourism operations occur in natural areas. In this way people can feel that they are really escaping from their normal lives. A person might experience heightened senses, an adrenalin rush or a sense of calm following the experience. Again, it is important to remember that adventure can mean different things to different people. Sailing a boat around the Greek Islands may seem adventurous to some but not to others.

Adventure Activities

Activities associated with adventure can be categorized into the following:

- Physical – e.g., hiking, mountain-biking and hang gliding.
- Nature-based – e.g., bushwalking, birdwatching.
- Cultural – e.g., pilgrimages.
- Travel/Exploration – e.g., long-distance sailing, Silk Road treks.

These activities form niche markets within the tourism industry based on the activity undertaken and their setting. They can vary in their "adventure" rating. Guided garden tours would be considered not to be very adventurous, whereas camping in the Andes would be considered extremely adventurous.

Nature-based tourism can fall into both categories of "ecotourism" and "adventure tourism". However, nature-based tourism would not necessarily be classed as "ecotourism". Ecotourism embraces the principles of sustainable tourism, concerning the economic, social and environmental impacts of tourism, and as such is more specifically determined than simply being nature-based tourism. The type of tourism will depend upon the location of the activity, remoteness and degree of difficulty.

Types of Adventure Tourism

Adventure tourism can refer to different ideas to certain people, adventure tourism refers to any type of adventure that requires you to participate in engaging cultural, physical or natural excursions with the aim of bringing the participants out of their comfort zones.

Adventure tourism consists of hard adventure, as well as soft adventure whereby hard adventure typically involves some form of danger or risk.

On the other hand, soft adventure simply opens you up to explore areas that other travellers would not. Such as visiting a relatively unknown nation.

Hot Air Ballooning

Hot air ballooning is one of the best to fully take in the bird's eye view of the place that you are visiting.

The views that you get can only be experienced from above and they will stay with you long after the trip is over.

Balloon rides are getting popular across the world. Few of the best Balloon rides in the world ensure that you get to bring back an experience of a lifetime.

Zip Lining

Zip lining has always been a hot adventure sport which means that it is easily available almost anywhere in the world.

Ziplining is perfect for travellers that are chasing a thrill without going too overboard.

Free Falling

When most people picture free falling, one of the foremost things that immediately come to mind is skydiving or bungee jumping. Yes, even those are pretty much a part of Adventure tourism.

Free falling is similar to both these activities but it has been specifically designed to give you the same feeling but with less risk involved.

So, if Bungee jumping or Skydiving is too adventurous for you, Free falling is something which you can try for sure.

Rafting

This is one of the most common, yet extremely popular, type of Adventure tourism. Rafting can be both a soft adventure and a hard one depending on the location that you are doing it in.

If you are looking for a hard adventure, you can satisfy your craving for adventure by battling big rapids.

However, if you are looking for a calmer adventure, then rafting later on in the season when the water levels are low might be more suitable.

Spelunking

Plainly put, spelunking or caving refers to the act of exploring caves for adventure purposes.

Spelunking is increasingly becoming a popular type of Adventure Tourism.

It consists of trying to climb squeeze and crawl through caves and tight passages.

Those looking for an adventure can also zip line or rappel down different cave levels or explore the underwater where possible.

BASE Jumping

BASE jumping is a type of adventure activity that allows individuals to jump off any one of these locations- Buildings, Antennas, Span, and the Earth (cliff).

Base jumping might involve activities such as jumping out of a speeding aeroplane at 15000 feet and free falling at over 100 mph.

Mountaineering

Mountaineering can also be hard or soft depending on your skill level, as well as the mountain that you are tackling.

Mountaineering can, therefore, involve something as basic as rock climbing or something as taxing as tackling a glacier or a rocky mountain in the Himalayas.

This has been probably the most popular form of adventure tourism over the years. Yet, interest and participation seem to have grown over the years.

Accessible Tourism

Accessible tourism is the ongoing endeavour to ensure tourist destinations, products and services are accessible to all people, regardless of their physical limitations, disabilities or age. It encompasses publicly and privately owned tourist locations. The term has been defined by Darcy and Dickson as:

> Accessible tourism enables people with access requirements, including mobility, vision, hearing and cognitive dimensions of access, to function independently and with equity and dignity through the delivery of universally designed tourism products, services and environments. This definition is inclusive of all people including those travelling with children in prams, people with disabilities and seniors.

Disabled persons in a museum.

Modern society is increasingly aware of the concept of integration of people with disabilities. Issues such as accessibility, design for all and universal design are featured in the international symposia of bodies such as the European Commission. Steps have been taken to promote guidelines and best practices, and major resources are now dedicated to this field.

Nehantic Trail - Rhododendron Sanctuary Trail entrance and Wheelchair-accessible sign.

A greater understanding of the accessible tourism market has been promoted through research commissioned by the European Commission where a stakeholder analysis has provided an insight into the complexities of accessible tourism. Similarly, the Australian Sustainable Tourism Cooperative Research Centre funded an Accessible Tourism Research Agenda that sought to outline a research base on which to develop the supply, demand and coordination/regulation information required to develop the market segment. The research agenda has now seen three other funded projects contribute towards a research base on which the tourism industry and government marketing authorities can make more informed decisions.

As of 2008, there were more than 50 million persons with disabilities in Europe, and more than 600 million around the world. When expanded to include all beneficiaries of accessible tourism, as defined above, the number grows to some 130 million people affected in Europe alone. over 1 billion of people in the world had some disability, of whom nearly 200 million experienced severe difficulty in functioning.

In addition to the social and health benefits, the market represents an opportunity for new investment and new service requirements, rarely provided by key players in the tourism sector.

According to ENAT, the European Network for Accessible Tourism, accessible tourism includes:

- Barrier-free destinations: Infrastructure and facilities.
- Transport: By air, land and sea, suitable for all users.
- High quality services: Delivered by trained staff.
- Activities, exhibits, attractions: Allowing participation in tourism by everyone.
- Marketing, booking systems, web sites & services: Information accessible to all.

Specific Needs and Requirements

Specific problems found by travellers or tourists with disabilities include:

- Inaccessible, or only partly accessible, web sites.

- Lack of accessible airport transfer.
- Lack of wheelchair accessible vehicles.
- Lack of well-adapted hotel rooms.
- Lack of professional staff capable of dealing with accessibility issues.
- Lack of reliable information about a specific attraction's level of accessibility.
- Lack of accessible restaurants, bars, and other facilities.
- Lack of adapted toilets in restaurants and public places.
- Inaccessible streets and sidewalks.
- Lack of technical aids and disability equipment such as wheelchairs, bath chairs and toilet raisers.

A campground picnic table made accessible to wheelchairs and walkers with its extended top.

An accessible "boardwalk" ramp with landings for stopping to enjoy a panorama view. Harris Beach State Park.

Kapiti Island coast accessible beach, wheelchair ramp, Paekakariki.

An accessible yurt shelter in Pinery Provincial Park.

Europe and the United States of America are home to the majority of the existing companies in this niche. However, companies worldwide are starting to appear as the result of a growing need, largely driven by senior tourism, due to increasing life expectancy in developed countries. The United States requires ADA compliant ramp access to virtually all businesses and public places.

An accessible shower stall at a State park.

Morgan's Wonderland is an accessible family amusement park, designed similar to a sensory garden with interactive games.

A wheelchair with adaptive tires for travelling across snow at a ski hill. Such chairs can be loaned or rented to users.

Portugal, Spain, the United Kingdom, Germany, France and other northern European countries are increasingly prepared to receive tourists in wheelchairs, and to provide disability equipment and wheelchair accessible transport.

With the growth of the internet, online travel planning is also becoming more common, leading to the rise of online accessibility maps. Starting in 2016, Lonely Planet started offering online resources by country.

Disaster Tourism

Disaster tourism at Mount Merapi.

Disaster tourism has been defined as the practice of visiting locations at which an environmental disaster, either natural or man-made, has occurred. Although a variety of disasters are the subject of subsequent disaster tourism, the most common disaster tourist sites are the areas surrounding volcanic eruptions. Opinions on the morality and impact of disaster tourism are divided. Advocates of disaster tourism often claim that the practice raises awareness of the event, stimulates the local economy, and educates the public about the local culture, while critics claim that the practice is exploitative, profits on loss, and often mischaracterizes the events in question.

Motivations of Disaster Tourists

The conventional motivations present in individuals practicing disaster tourism. Attraction is typically derived from personal connection in a social, academic or cultural essence. Another population of visitors hope to aid in providing relief to the affected areas—some directly through volunteer work and some indirectly through donations. Other visitors have no connection to the site or the event, but happen to be there as tourists and visit those places as part of their sightseeing. A common example of this is tourists who come to Italy to sightsee in Rome and end up visiting Pompeii and its neighboring cities without initially intending to do so.

Reception of Disaster Tourism

Disaster tourism has had a mixed reception, with critics labelling it as voyeuristic and profiting off of loss and with advocates arguing that the tourism stimulates the recovering economy and brings awareness to local culture. Although the public perception of tourism depends on a wide variety of factors, such whether the disaster was man-made or natural and how long it has been since the incident, there are some general trends in the reception of tourism.

Depending on the site or tour, disaster tourism can be seen to be an educational experience or exploitative. Whether or not a tourist site is handled in a respectful and tactful manner often is determined both by those organizing the events and the tourists themselves. Moreover, advocates of disaster tourism point out that attractions are capable of re-examining disasters in an educational manner despite that the operators are motivated by profit. Many of these advocates argue that when distasteful disaster tourism occurs, the blame lies primarily on the tourists for providing an insensitive demand rather on the operators for fulfilling such a demand. For both tourists and operators, however, parsing the difference between an educational and an exploitative one requires asking what areas are crucial for understanding the disaster and clarifying how behavior that is appropriate in a destroyed area is often different from behavior that is appropriate in newly built homes or temporary camps.

The effect of tourism on the local economy is often nuanced due to the specifics in how tourism affects local income. It is generally accepted that if the tours comprise public events organized by volunteers, then there are consistent but small increases to charity donations. However, if the tours are organized by private companies, then it is not always clear how what proportion of the profits go back into relief efforts. Furthermore, while governmental regulation typically prevents private tours from slowing down or reversing reconstruction in areas where reconstruction has already began, critics argue that private touring may deincentivize the reconstruction of locations and sites, in which reconstruction has yet to occur. Another possible situation is that the tours are not organized by formal entities but instead by less cohesive groups of citizens. These cases are relatively unstudied due to their rarity.

Similarly, visiting disaster sites is thought to have an effect on empathy, but the nature of the effect it has depends on the particulars of the visit. Unorganized visits, for example, can often raise empathy by forcing the visitors to see suffering up close and prompting them to consider how to interact with victims. More organized visits, on the other hand, have been accused of lowering empathy because they comprised tourists "acting like tourists and dressing like tourists," which dilutes and sanitizes the experience.

Virtual Reality in Disaster Tourism

Facebook's Virtual Tour of Puerto Rico

In September 2017, Hurricane Maria devastated the Dominican Republic and Puerto Rico. Hurricane Maria is estimated to caused 4,645 deaths total, and in Puerto Rico, it is estimated to have caused $94 billion in property damage and displaced approximately 60,000 people.

On October 9, 2017, Facebook CEO Mark Zuckerberg and Facebook social VR chief Rachel Franklin used a livestream to showcase Facebook's new VR app, Facebook Spaces, by taking a virtual tour of the devastated areas Puerto Rico. During the 10 minute video, Zuckerberg explains how Facebook partnered with Red Cross to build population map from satellite imagery and better allocate the relief effort.

The public reception to the tour was unanimously negative. Zuckerberg drew criticism for describing VR as "magical" in its ability to transport people to disaster zones, and most viewers considered the cartoon avatars of Zuckerberg and Franklin to be an inappropriately jovial tone. The day following the livestream, Zuckerberg apologized, explaining, "When you're in VR yourself, the surroundings feel quite real. But that sense of empathy doesn't extend well to people watching you as a virtual character on a 2D screen."

Examples of Disaster Tourism

79 AD Eruption of Mt Vesuvius

When the nearby volcano Mt Vesuvius erupted in 79 AD, the eruption buried the city of Pompeii and the nearby city of Herculaneum and preserved everything from its streets to its frescoes under mounds of pumice and ash. Although Pompeii was initially rediscovered in 1599, tourism was undesirable until Spanish engineer Rocque Joaquin de Alcubierre performed a much larger excavation in 1748, which revealed many noteworthy structures, such as a fully intact Roman theatre.

Today, Pompeii belongs to the much larger Vesuvius National Park and is one of Italy's most popular tourist sites, attracting approximately 2.5 million visitors annually.

Hindenburg Incident

In the early evening of May 6, 1937, the German passenger airship LZ 129 Hindenburg burst into flame during a docking attempt at the Lakehurst Naval Air Station, just outside Lakehurst, New Jersey. With the cause of the fire unknown and a death toll of thirty-seven passengers, the Hindenburg disaster became one of the biggest news stories of its time.

Today, a bronze plaque and cement outline the site of the incident. Immediately east of the crash site, volunteers of the Navy Lakehurst Historical Society will conduct public tours of Historic Hangar One, the location where the Hindenburg was kept.

Chernobyl Nuclear Plant Explosion

On the morning of April 26, 1986, the number four reactor of the Chernobyl nuclear power plant exploded, producing airborne radioactive materials and a fire that burned for ten days. The Chernobyl explosion caused dozens of direct deaths and thousands of deaths due to long-term exposure. In the aftermath, 350,000 residents were displaced from Chernobyl and the nearby city of Pripyat. The other three reactors at Chernobyl power plant continued running at the time but were gradually lessened until the power plant's shutdown in 2000.

The Ukraine-based tour company SoloEast Travel currently runs daylong tours through Chernobyl's exclusion zone, a thousand square-mile area that includes the plant. The highlights of the tour include visiting Red Forest, a pine tree woodland destroyed by radioactive contamination, exploring Kopachi, a nearby village that was demolished due to high contamination levels, and finally coming within 1000 feet of the remains of the number four reactor. These tours are met with some controversy because despite that SoloEast Travel claims that publicly accessible areas surrounding the power plant contain low levels of radiation and are deemed safe, a number of third party scientists disagree.

Exxon Valdez Oil Spill

In 1989, the *Exxon Valdez* oil tanker struck Alaska's Bligh Reef in Prince William Sound and leaked crude oil into the sound. An estimated 30 million plus gallons spilled. Oil from the spill would eventually contaminate more than 11,000 square-miles of ocean and 1300 miles of coastline. The spill killed hundreds of sea otters, harbor seals, and eagles and hundreds of thousands of seabird in the days following the spill. Despite that it is not the world's largest oil spill, the *Exxon Valdez* oil spill is typically considered the most notorious in American history.

Having been among the first responders, the family-run Stan Stephens Cruises operates glacier tours out of Prince William Sound that highlight the history surrounding the Exxon Valdez spill and its aftermath.

Hurricane Katrina

In late August 2005, Hurricane Katrina devastated the American city of New Orleans. Although 80–90% of the population was evacuated prior, twenty-three breaches in navigational canal levees, drainage canal levees, and floodwalls occurred as a result of Katrina's storm surge. With these failures, 80% of New Orleans became flooded, which in turn caused over 200,000 homes to be destroyed and 800,000 residents to be displaced. At the time, the disaster had a large impact on the politics, population, and economics for a sizable portion of the United States.

A decade after the incident, the effects of Hurricane Katrina are still visible and catastrophic. Although many companies offer bus tours of the still-damaged regions, critics argues that these tours interfere with the relief effort. Some have suggested that curious tourists should instead go on bike tours in order to restrict the disruption to residents trying to get their lives back on track. Quite frequently, tours will focus on showcasing the culture of specific districts and neighborhood, treating Hurricane Katrina as the most recent event in a much longer cultural history. Many tours donate their profits or a portion of their profits to local relief organizations.

Eruption of Eyjafjallajökull

Eyjafjallajökull, in Iceland, began erupting on 20 March 2010. At this time, about 500 farmers and their families from the areas of Fljótshlíð, Eyjafjöll, and Landeyjar were evacuated overnight, but allowed to return to their farms and homes after Civil Protection Department risk assessment. On 14 April 2010, Eyjafjallajökull erupted for the second time, requiring 800 people to be evacuated.

In the wake of the first eruption, tour companies offered trips to see the volcano. However, the ash cloud from the second eruption disrupted air traffic over Great Britain and most of northern and western Europe, making it difficult to travel to Iceland even though Iceland's airspace itself remained open throughout.

Eruption of Mt Merapi

In the November of 2010, the active Indonesian volcano of Mt Merapi had its second eruption in a century, which led to direct deaths of 353 people and the displacement of approximately 400,000 people in nearby villages.

Mt Merapi is unique among disaster tourist sites because Merapi was a popular tourist site prior to the volcano's eruption, and tourism had already made up a significant portion of the local economy. While many tour companies and travel agencies hold more standard sightseeing tours of the affected areas, some programs provide more direct paths to donating to local charities and getting involved in the relief effort. For example, the Go Green Campaign encourages tourists to purchase small trees or seeds and plant them in local villages.

Jungle Tourism

Jungle tourism is a subcategory of adventure travel defined by active multifaceted physical means of travel in the jungle regions of the earth. Although similar in many respects to adventure travel, jungle tourism pertains specifically to the context of region, culture and activity. According to the Glossary of Tourism Terms, jungle tours have become a major component of green tourism in tropical destinations and are a relatively recent phenomenon of Western international tourism.

Of the regions that take part in tourism-driven sustainable development practices and eco tourism, Mexican, Central and South American practices are the most pervasive in the industry; notably Mayan jungle excursions. Other regions include jungle territories in Africa, Australia, and the South Pacific.

Central and South America

Chichen Itza.

The Tikal.

Copán.

The majority of jungle tour operators are concentrated in what is known as the Mayan World or "Ruta Maya". The Mayan World encompasses five different countries that hosted the entirety of the Mayan Civilization: Mexico, Guatemala, Belize, Honduras and El Salvador. Most tours consist of visits to popular Mayan archaeological sites such as Tikal, Guatemala, Chichen Itza, and Copan. These day visits will usually consist of a guided tour of a heavily tourist-concentrated Mayan and archaeological site. Tikal and Chichen Itza are prime examples of popular day-visit sites. Such sites involve a tour guide, designated either by the state government or by a private company, for the tourists. These tour guides are predominantly trained professionals, certified to take large parties of fifty through heavily populated archaeological sites. Nicaragua and Costa Rica are also popular destinations for this type of adventure travel.

Although most of the visits to these more prominent sites involve day trips, there are also many jungle tour operators that showcase less-known, remote Mayan jungle ruins such as Nakum, Yax-ha, and El Mirador. These tours involve much more preparation, time and funding to explore as they are usually in very remote and generally inaccessible regions of the Mayan jungles. These ruins and sites are reached by alternative and physically taxing means of travel such as bicycle, canoe, horseback or hiking. This is what essentially differentiates jungle tourism from any other sort of adventure travel tours. There are several tour operators that will employ the use of machetes during tours.

Another difference is that the majority of tour operators that travel deep into the Central and South American jungle will cap the number of persons traveling in the group at ten to fifteen. This is done to minimize the impact on the jungle flora and fauna. Federal laws in some countries prohibit any given group larger than fifteen people traveling through the Mayan jungle, a generally protected region, but limited resources for enforcing such laws have allowed such practices to occur under the radar.

In Guatemala it has become very popular to hike through the jungle of the Mayan Biosphere due to the discovery of El Mirador, also known as the Lost City of Maya. There are no roads. Many take a quick flight from Flores while others hike through the jungles of the department of Petén. Groups should be smaller than 15 people in order to reduce the impact on the environment.

6

Components of Tourism and Travel Industry

Tourism is a vast domain comprising of several components that facilitate it. These are tourism transportation, travel agency, tourist attraction, tour operator, travel agency, etc. The topics elaborated in this chapter will help in gaining a better perspective about all the components of tourism and travel industry.

Tourism is the business of attracting visitors and catering to their needs and expectations. The following is an overview of the major components of the tourism and travel industry.

Tourist Destinations

- Government promotion offices.
- Regional promotion offices.
- Resort areas, convention centers.

Transportation

- Airlines:
    - Major.
    - National.
    - Regional.
    - Nonscheduled /charter.
- Ground Transporte:
    - Rent-a-car.
    - Motor/coach.
    - Railroad.

Accommodation

- Hotels.
- Motels.
- Resorts.
- Cruise lines.

Tourist Attractions

- Attractions.
- Theme parks.
- Museums.

Travel Brokers

- Travel agents.
- Travel wholesalers.
- Tour and charter operators.
- Ground operators.
- Travel incentive companies.

Travel Related Services

- Financial (credit cards, travellers cheques, travel insurance).
- Travel publications guide books.

Our world is diverse. It is composed of countries with a variety of cultures and customs, rural areas and urban centers, each with its own distinct flavor, and so on.

The activity we call tourism, with its great economic and social benefits, provides citizens of all countries with an opportunity to explore new places, to meet new people, to learn new things, and, perhaps in the process, learn more about themselves.

Travel is a bridge between people. It makes a valuable contribution to the world's economy, employs more people than any other industry and affects the lives of all in one way or another.

Today, the terms tourism and travel have become almost interchangeable. However, when we look at the history of transporting people, we see that in the early days travel was a far from a pleasurable activity.

The word "tourism" a relatively new addition to the English language, introduced only in the nineteenth century. It connotes the act of travelling for pleasure, as well as the industry that developed to service that activity.

Tourism also connotes the ability of people to escape from familiar surroundings and everyday routine. It is no wonder, then that the history of tourism is the history of those who broadened the horizons of transportation.

It was those who dreamed and those who dared, including Henry Ford and the Wright brothers, who gave us our present day transportation system which harmoniously links speed, safety and economy.

While travel has been a human passion since the dawn of history, tourism only became possible as technological improvements provided comfortable, safe, and, above all, enjoyable ways to travel.

The modern tourism industry is composed of numerous separate industry segments. Sometimes competing, yet more often providing services supplementary in nature. Each segment of the industry developed as a result of different historical forces.

Tourism Transportation

The transport industry has gained a vital place in the global network system and is one of the most important components of the tourism infrastructure. It now becomes easier for people to travel from one place to another because of the various modes of transportation available.

The earliest forms of transportation in the ancient times were animals on land and sails on the sea. Travel development from the need to survive, to expand and develop trade to far off countries, and the hunger to capture new lands and territories. This was followed by the use of steams and electricity in the nineteenth century followed by internal combustion engines.

Aircraft with the jet engines were introduced in the 1950s. With the development of technology, travel became faster and more and people could travel around the globe.

Since tourism involves the movement of people from their places of residence to the places of tourist attractions, every tourist has to travel to reach the places of interest. Transport is, thus, one of the major components of the tourism industry. To develop any place of tourist attraction there have to be proper, efficient, and safe modes of transportation.

Transportation is vital to tourism. Studies have shown that tourists spend almost 30 to 40 percent of their total holiday expenditure on transportation and the remaining on food, accommodation, and other activities. This aspect once again highlights the importance of transportation.

A tourist can travel by a variety of means. The tourism professional, as well as tourist, should be aware of the various modes of transport available to reach the destination and at the destination.

The various mode of transport can be broadly divided into the following three categories:

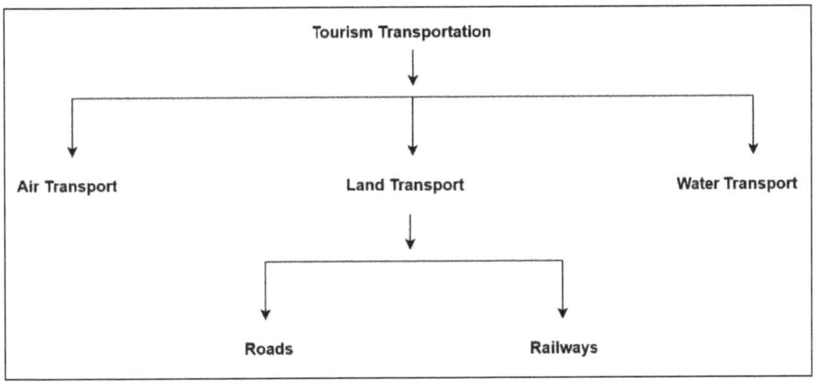

- Air transport,
- Land transport,
- Water transport.

Air Transport

Due to the growth of air transport in recent years, long-distance travel has become much simpler and affordable. Distance is now measured in hours and not in kilometers. The world has indeed shrunk and becomes a small village.

The development of air transport mostly occurred after World War I and II. Commercial airlines were created for travelers. Because of increasing air traffic, the commercial sector grows rapidly. Before the World War II, Swissair already was carrying around 14-16 passenger between Zurich to London.

The first commercial service was introduced by KLM, the Dutch Airlines, in 1920 between Amsterdam and London. Commercial air travel grew mostly after World War II. More facilities were introduced and there was more comfort in travel.

Jet flights were inaugurated by Great Britain in the year 1952. In the year 1958 Pan American introduced the Boeing 707 services between Paris and New York. Due to the introduction of jet flights, the year 1959 onward saw a tremendous increase in air traffic. The concept of chartered flights was also introduced during this year.

Jumbo jets have revolutionized travel. A large number of people travel by air because of the speed, comfort, and economy in terms of time saved.

The modern era, thus, is the era of mass air travel. After road transport, air travel is the most popular mode of travel, particularly for international travel. For the business travelers, air transport is more convenient as it saves their precious time and offers a luxurious and hassle-free travel. Many airlines nowadays offer special facilities to the business tourist such as Internet on board.

There two types of airlines. These are following as:

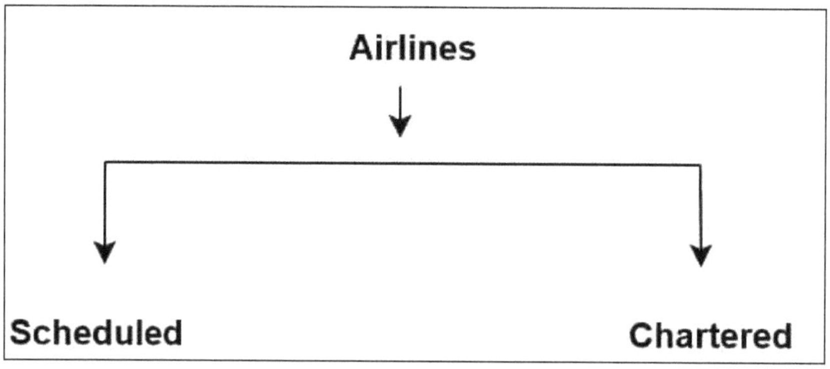

- Scheduled,
- Chartered.

Scheduled airlines operate as regular schedules. Chartered airlines or the non-scheduled airlines operate only when there is a demand, mainly during the tourist seasons. The chartered flights work out cheaper than the scheduled carriers as they are operated only when there is a high load factor. Chartered flights provide cheaper packages to the destination such as Portugal and Spain.

The International Air Transport Association (IATA) regulates international air travel. IATA has more than 105 major airlines of the world as its members. IATA regulates the price of tickets on different sectors of travel in the world. The concerned government decides the domestic fares.

The airfares are normally determined on the volume and the air travel demand in an area.

The International Civil Aviation Organization (ICAO) is an intergovernmental organization established in the year 1945. Only the government of the country can become a member. The government has to enter into a bilateral agreement for the frequency of flights for operating commercial airlines between them.

Airlines are classified into two broad categories namely small carrier and large carrier. The small carrier also known as commuter airlines have less than 30 seats. The larger carriers, also known as major airlines fly direct routes between the major cities and seat and seat 100 to 800 passengers.

The recent boom in the aviation technology has certainly bought some new development to airlines industry. There has been a major change in the size of the aircraft.

Every year there are a growing number of new airlines being introduced. Because of the growing number of new private airlines, there is stiff competition among them. This has resulted in a considerable reduction in air fairs and has boosted the growth of air traffic. To woo and attract customers, many airlines offer cheaper promotional fares such as excursion fares, group fares, and apex fares.

Million of tonnes of cargo and mail are also handled by the air transport industry.

Road Transport

Humans travel place to place in search of food in the primitive era. They tamed animals such as the dog, ox, horse, camel, reindeer, elephants, etc. for carrying the load and traveling. After the discovery of the wheel, humans developed the cart, the chariot, and the carriage.

Until the seventeenth century, horses were used for traveling. Later on better roads were constructed and some of these roads developed into trade routes, which linked many countries. One of them is the Silk Route which was used for transporting silk from China to Persia and the Blue Gem road from Iran to Afghanistan and India.

Today, the most popular and widely used mode of road travel is the automobile or the car. Road transport is dominated by the automobile, which provides views of the landscape and the freedom to travel. Tourist often travels with their entire family for holidays.

To promote tourism, the vehicle required are coaches and tourist cars. Tourist coaches or buses are preferred for large tourist groups traveling together on a specified tour itinerary. Many tourists prefer to travel in comfort and privacy and hire cars. Cars of various makes and standards are available on a rental basis.

Tourist also uses their own motorcar when holidaying. Cars and coaches carried long distance by train facility is also available in some countries.

The car rental segment of the tourism industry is in a very advanced stage in foreign countries. The client can book a car, himself or through agents, and make it wait at the desired place at the destination. The client can then drive the car himself /herself on reaching the destination.

Rail Transport

The railway is the most economical, convenient, and popular mode of travel especially for long distance travel all over the world. The railroad was invented in the seventeenth century in Germany with wooden tracks. The first steel rail was developed in the USA during the early 1800s. The railways revolutionized transportation and mass movement of people seen in the nineteenth and twentieth centuries.

The broad gauge lines account for more than 55 percent of the total network and carry 85 percent of total traffic. The steam engines have been replaced by diesel and electric engines which have helped in increasing the speed. Railways have promoted tourism by introducing a special tourist train.

In Europe, the railway systems of six European countries have been clubbed to make rail travel easier for the people of Europe. A rail passenger can buy a ticket in any one country of Europe and travel through six countries. For the foreign tourists, Eurail Passes offer unlimited discounts travel in express trains for periods ranging from a week to three months. In the USA, AMTRAK operates trains.

Water Transport

Humans have been traveling through water since time immemorial and carried good and people from one place to another. The boats progressed from the simple raft with some modifications and improvement and were first used around 6000 BC.

Travel by ship was the only means for traveling overseas until the middle of the twentieth century. The Cunard Steamship Company was formed in 1838 with regular steamship services operating on the North Atlantic. During the World War I, in 1914 the operations of the steamship company had to be suspended. After the World War I, the steamship luxury liners were back to business till World War II.

After the World War II, the large luxury liners again started their operations all over the world and carried passengers and holidaymakers. Some of the linear were very large accommodating up to 1000 passengers and had facilities like swimming pools, cinema halls, shops, casino, etc.

The cruise lines are the new attraction among the tourist. The cruises are booked several months in advance for trips into the tropical and sub-tropical waters of the Hawaii, Caribbean, Mediterranean, etc. Water transport today plays two main roles in travel and tourism namely ferrying and cruising.

Modern vessels such as the wave -piercing, the hydrofoil and the hovercraft are the over the water transport and used for short distance routes.

Water transportation is also used in riverboat travel. The Mississippi River has been a popular tourist river since the first settlers came to the USA. Today, tourists enjoy two or three-day luxury trips along the river. In Europe, the Rhine, winding through the grapes growing areas of Germany, offers similar leisure tourist trips.

Motorized ferries and launches are used over rivers to transport tourists and locals, to transport vehicles, and offer facilities such as car parking, restaurants, viewing decks, etc.

Advantages and Disadvantages of Various Modes of Transport

Tourist has a wide variety of transport options available today. There are several advantages and disadvantages of all the model of transport. These are following as:

Air Transport

Direct root, high speed, quick service, social and political significance, luxurious travel are the advantages of air transportation.

High cost, jet lag, unsuitable for heavy bulk cargo, accidents always fatal, international rule to be observed are the disadvantages of air transportation.

Road Transport

Flexibility, reliable, door to door service, economical, supplements other modes of transport, quick transit for short distances are the advantages of road transport.

Slow speed, carrying capacity limited, accidents, none- AC coaches not so comfortable, comfort depends upon the conditions of roads are the disadvantages of road transport.

Railways

Long distance travel cheaper, carrying capacity large, dependable service, quicker than road transportation, ability to view scenery en route is the advantage of railways.

Inflexible, unfit to hilly regions, difficulties in rural areas, dining car facilities not always available are the disadvantage of railways.

Water Transport

Economical, carrying capacity enormously, develops international and coastal trades are the advantages of water transport.

Transport as an Attraction

To attract customers as well as take them around an attraction, destination developers have used many forms of transport to move people around. These novel modes of transport ensure that major exhibits are viewed in a certain sequence and ensure that the crowd moves through at a reliable pace.

Overcrowding should be avoided at all costs to prevent untoward incidents and to maintain the beauty of the place. Tourist can cover the entire park in a shorter duration with the help of these modes of transport.

Transportation is the most crucial component of the tourism infrastructure. It is required not only for reaching the destination but also visiting the site and moving about at the destination. Variety in modes of transportation adds color to the overall tourism experience.

Unusual forms of transportation are also an attraction such as the cable cars in hilly terrain, the funicular railway, or jet boating. The choice of mode of transport is vast and tourists can choose a mode to suit their budget. They can opt for scheduled or non-scheduled transport such as the hiring of vehicles, boats, coaches or trains so that they can travel with their group.

Travel Agency

Travel agent is a person who has a full knowledge about tourists product – destinations, modes of travel, climate, accommodation and other areas of the service sector. He acts on the behalf of product providers/principles and in return get a commission. Technically, a travel agent is an owner or manager of an agency, but other employees are responsible for advising tourists and selling packages tours/individual components of travel products.

A travel agent may be an individual /firm or corporation which is commonly known as a travel agency. An agency means the office of travel agent or organization where all travel goods and services are assembled and coordinated for the smooth conduct of travel agency business.

Travel agency is one of the most important organization in the tourism private sector which plays a significant and crucial role in the entire process of developing and promoting tourism in the country or at a destination. It is a travel agency which packages and processes all the attractions, accesses, amenities and ancillary services of a country and present them to tourists. That's why travel agency is known as 'image builder' of a country.

A prospective travel agency is one which makes arrangements of travel tickets (air, rail, road, and sea); travel documents (passports, visa and other documents required to travel); accommodation, entertainment, and other travel-related services from principle suppliers. It may also secure travel insurance, foreign currency for traveling people.

Types of Travel Agency

Travel agencies are basically categories in two types-: Retail Travel Agency and Wholesale Travel Agency.

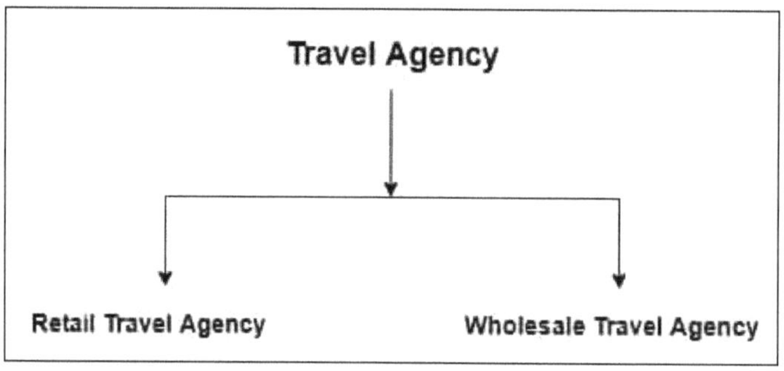

Retail Travel Agency

A retail travel agency sells tourists products directly to the public on the behalf of the products suppliers and in return get commissions. Some package tour is sold in two ways i.e., on a commission basis and mark up the price.

When a travel agency sells a tour on the marked-up price it means that first, it markup the cost of the tour and then sell it at a higher rate. The markup price is the difference between retail price and wholesale cost.

Wholesale Travel Agency

These agencies are specialized in organizing package tours, which are marketed to the customers/tourists through the network of a retail travel agency or directly to the prospective clients (if wholesale travel agency has a retail division). A wholesale travel agency purchases tourists product components in the bulk and designs tour package.

Sometimes, a wholesale travel agency buys travel components from the vendor in bulk and resell them to another travel business originations.

Wholesale travel agencies assemble package holidays and sell them to the clients through retail travel agencies. A typical package tour includes – air tickets, accommodation, and something other services may also be included in it such as entertainment, sightseeing, and sports activities etc.

These packages are referred to as 'package tours' most of these tours include the services of escorts but a few are sold to people who wish to travel independently.

Generally, a wholesaler receives volume discounts from the principal suppliers because a wholesaler might agree to purchase a large number of seats from a particular airline or reserve a large number of room at a particular hotel or resorts.

Practically, a wholesaler who sells package vacations/tours is called a Tour Operator. However, technically there is a difference between a wholesaler and a tour operator. A wholesaler who sells tourists product individually without assembling them into a package tour is called as a Consolidator.

Mostly, these are specialized in particular product components such as air tickets, accommodation, and conference, and conventions etc.

Difference between Wholesale Travel Agencies and Tour Operators

The wholesale travel agencies may offer or operate the package tours or may specialize in developing tours for inbound as well as outbound travelers. They are often referred to as tour operators, but these two essentially different:

- Wholesale travel agency does not sell directly to the public, while tour operators do sell directly to clients.
- A wholesale travel agency usually combines, assembles and contacts for existing travel services to formulate a new travel product she has his own one or more components of travel product i.e., ' inclusive tours.'
- Wholesale travel agencies are less inclined than tour operators to perform ground services i.e. handling agency or ground operators.
- A wholesale travel agency may deal with one component of travel product while a tour operator offers a variety of tour programmes.
- The size of the business is large in the case of tour operators in comparison to a wholesale travel agency.

Features and Importance of the Travel Agency

Travel agency plays an important role in travel sector business. Some most important features and importance of the travel agency business are as follows:

- An important link between the clients and principal suppliers.

- Image-Builder.
- Ensures rapid travel services.
- Provider of an authentic and reliable travel information.
- A social a continuous process.
- Establishes a good relationship with clients and vendors.

These are the most important features of the Travel Agency Business.

Functions and Services of Travel Agency

Today, Travel Agencies have been recognized as a vital component of travel and tourism and have become an integral part of the travel and tourism industry at global. They account for more than 90% of international and 70% of domestic tourist traffic.

Further, more than 60% of all travel agency revenues are derived from business travel. Most travel agencies sell both commercial and leisure travel but there are many travel agencies which only specialized in one sector or the other.

The operation of each travel agency is based on the scope of its activities and organizational size. The main function of large-scale travel agency are:

Travel Information

Whatever the size of a travel agency, it has to provide necessary travel information to tourists. A travel agency must give up-to-date, accurate and timely information regarding destinations mode of travel, accommodation, sight-seeing, shopping, immigration, passport, visa, customs clearance and procedure, health and security rules and about various permits required to travel in particular areas etc.

Itinerary Preparation

The term tourists itinerary is used to identify the origin, destination and all the stopping points in a traveler's tours. It is a composition of various elements and designed after a detailed study of the market. Travel agencies prepare an itinerary for tour packages.

Airline Ticketing and Reservation

A travel agency sells a variety of tourism products. Airline ticketing and reservation is still a major source of revenue. Travel agencies perform a function of airline ticketing and reservation on the behalf of various airlines.

Tour Packaging and Costing

Travel agencies prepare tour package and sell them to tourists. The coasting and pricing of tour packages depend to a large extent on the ability of travel agent as to how effectively he is able to negotiate with the principal suppliers.

Reservation

It is a very important function of all types of travel agencies. A travel agency consistently makes linkage with the accommodation sector, transport sector and other entertainment organizations to reserve rooms, and seats in the cultural programmes and transportation.

Travel Insurance

Some large-scale travel agencies perform additional functions to serve its clients. Travel insurance protects the travelers against the personal as well as baggage losses resulting from a wide range of travel related happenings and problems.

Currency Services

Approved travel agency authorized by Govt. body provides currency exchanges services to tourist.

Organisation of Conference/Conventions

Large-scale travel agencies offer a complete convention/conference package which includes registration of the participants at the venue to be picked up for dropped to the airport/hotel, overhead projectors, slide projectors, TV, VCR, information counter, sightseen etc.

Travel Agency Linkages and Integration

Basically, a travel agency serves two type of clients: business travelers and leisure travelers. Incidentally, the requirements of these tourists are different and an agency has to assemble or purchase related components from the principal suppliers to cater to their needs.

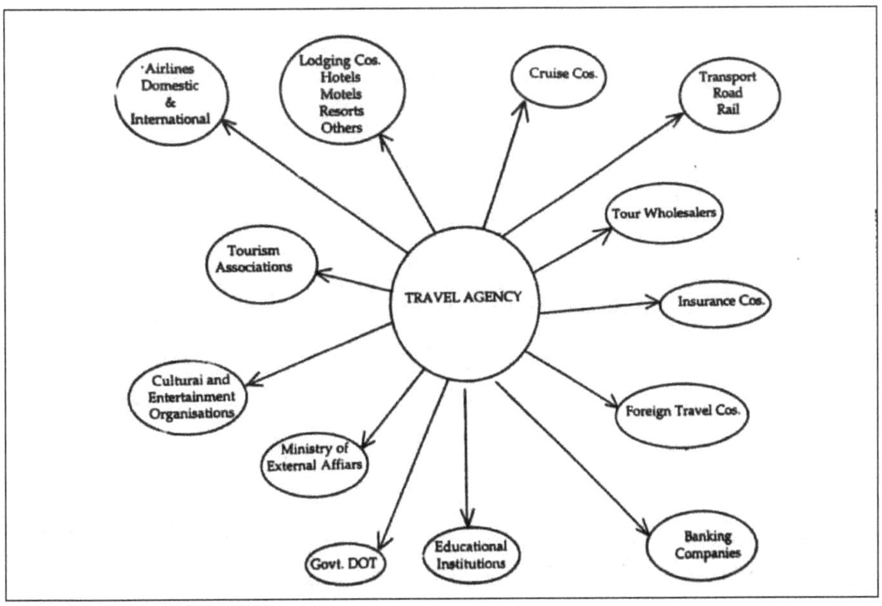

Essentially, travel agencies maintain close ties with Airlines, hotels, car rentals, banks, insurance companies, railways, government, trade associations, foreign tour operators and travel agents, ground operators, cruise companies and tourism educational institutes.

Tourist Attraction

A tourist attraction is a place of interest where tourists visit, typically for its inherent or an exhibited natural or cultural value, historical significance, natural or built beauty, offering leisure and amusement.

The Eiffel Tower, a popular tourist attraction. Almost 7 million visit the tower each year.

The Christ the King statue, has become a popular tourist attraction.

The Taj Mahal, a popular tourist attraction. More than 7-8 million visit the Taj Mahal each year.

Types

Places of natural beauty such as beaches, tropical island resorts, national parks, mountains, deserts and forests, are examples of traditional tourist attractions which people may visit. Cultural tourist attractions can include historical places, monuments, ancient temples, zoos, aquaria, museums and art galleries, botanical gardens, buildings and structures (such as forts, castles, libraries, former prisons, skyscrapers, bridges), theme parks and carnivals, living history museums, public art (sculptures, statues, murals), signs, ethnic enclave communities, historic trains and cultural events. Factory tours, industrial heritage, creative art and crafts workshops are the object of cultural niches like industrial tourism and creative tourism. Many tourist attractions are also landmarks.

Tropical beaches and Balinese culture are attractions that draw tourists to this popular island resort, such as Melasti rituals performed on the beach.

Tourist attractions are also created to capitalize on legends such as a supposed UFO crash site near Roswell, New Mexico and the alleged Loch Ness monster sightings in Scotland. Ghost sightings also make tourist attractions.

Ethnic communities may become tourist attractions, such as Chinatowns in the United States and the black British neighbourhood of Brixton in London, England.

In the United States, owners and marketers of attractions advertise tourist attractions on billboards along the sides of highways and roadways, especially in remote areas. Tourist attractions often distribute free promotional brochures to be displayed in rest areas, information centers, fast food restaurants, and motel rooms or lobbies.

While some tourist attractions provide visitors a memorable experience for a reasonable admission charge or even for free, others may be of low quality and overprice their goods and services (such as admission, food, and souvenirs) in order to profit excessively from tourists. Such places are commonly known as tourist traps.

Within cities, rides on boats and sightseeing buses are sometimes popular.

Novelty Attractions

Novelty attractions are oddities such as the "biggest ball of twine" in Cawker City, Kansas, the Corn Palace in Mitchell, South Dakota, or Carhenge in Alliance, Nebraska, where old cars serve in the place of stones in a replica of Stonehenge. Novelty attractions are not limited to the American Midwest, but are part of Midwestern culture.

Tourist Destination

A tourist destination is a city, town, or other area that is dependent to a significant extent on revenues from tourism, or "a country, state, region, city, or town which is marketed or markets itself as a place for tourists to visit". It may contain one or more tourist attractions and possibly some "tourist traps". Fátima town, for example, is a popular tourist destination in Portugal. Siem Reap town is a popular tourist destination in Cambodia, mainly owing to its proximity to the Angkor temples. The Loire valley, the third tourist destination in France, is a good example of a region marketed and branded as a place for tourists to visit, mainly known for its Châteaux of the Loire valley.

A tropical island resort is an island or archipelago that depends on tourism as its source of revenue. The Bahamas in the Caribbean, Bali in Indonesia, Phuket in Thailand, Hawaii in the United States, Palawan in the Philippines, Fiji in the Pacific, and Santorini and Ibiza in the Mediterranean are examples of popular island resorts.

France, the United States, and Spain were the three most popular international destinations in 2017. The total number of international travelers arriving in those countries was about 234 million, contributing 8.9%, 7.7%, and 14.9%, respectively, to the total GDP of those countries.

From the tourism industry supply perspective a destination is usually defined by a geo-political boundary, and destination marketing is most commonly funded by governments. From the traveler perspective, a destination might be perceived quite differently.

Economic Impact

The tourism generates substantial economic benefits for both host countries and tourists' home countries. Especially in developing countries, one of the primary motivations for a region to promote itself as a tourism destination is the expected economic benefit. According to the World Tourism Organization, 698 million people travelled to a foreign country in 2000, spending more than US$478 billion. International tourism receipts combined with passenger transport currently total more than US$575 billion – making tourism the world's number one export earner.

Tourist attractions can:

- Contribute to government revenues; direct contributions are generated by taxes on incomes from tourism employment and tourism businesses, and by direct levies on tourists, such as departure taxes.
- Provide employment.
- Support conservation of habitats, species and historic sites.
- Stimulate infrastructure investment.
- Contribute to local economies.
- Provide foreign currency earnings.

Some examples of tourist attractions are:

- Forests, national parks and reserves of flora and fauna.
- Communities of different ethnicity.
- Constructions and structures (old prisons, libraries, castles, bridges, skyscrapers) and historical places.
- Cultural and sports events.
- Public art.
- Art galleries and museums.
- Botanical gardens and zoos.
- Monuments.
- Theme parks.
- Historical trains and ships.
- Viewpoints.
- Restaurants.
- Concerts.

Tour Operator

A tour operator typically combines tour and travel components to create a package holiday. They advertise and produce brochures to promote their products, holidays and itineraries.

An open top double decker bus is used worldwide to provide sightseeing tours.

The most common example of a tour operator's product would be a flight on a charter airline plus a transfer from the airport to a hotel and the services of a local representative, all for one price. each tour operators may specialise in destinations, e.g. Italy, activities and experiences, e.g., skiing, or a combination thereof.

The original *raison d'être* of tour operating was the difficulty for ordinary folk of making arrangements in far-flung places, with problems of language, currency and communication. The advent of the Internet has led to a rapid increase in self-packaging of holidays. However, tour operators still have their competence in arranging tours for those who do not have time to do DIY holidays, and specialize in large group events and meetings such as conferences or seminars. Also, tour operators still exercise contracting power with suppliers (airlines, hotels, other land arrangements, cruise companies and so on) and influence over other entities (tourism boards and other government authorities) in order to create packages and special group departures for destinations that might otherwise be difficult and expensive to visit.

Travel Agency

A travel agency is a private retailer or public service that provides travel and tourism related services to the public on behalf of suppliers such as activities, airlines, car rentals, cruise lines, hotels, railways, travel insurance, and package tours. In addition to dealing with ordinary tourists, most travel agencies have a separate department devoted to making travel arrangements for business travelers; some travel agencies specialize in commercial and business travel only. There are also travel agencies that serve as general sales agents for foreign travel companies, allowing them to have offices in countries other than where their headquarters are located.

Operations

A travel agency's main function is to act as an agent, selling travel products and services on behalf of a supplier. Consequently, unlike other retail businesses, they do not keep a stock in hand, unless they have pre-booked hotel rooms and/or cabins on a cruise ship for a group travel event such as a wedding, honeymoon, or a group event. A package holiday or a ticket is not purchased from a supplier unless a customer requests that purchase. The holiday or ticket is supplied to the agency at a discount. The profit is therefore the difference between the advertised price which the customer pays and the discounted price at which it is supplied to the agent. This is known as the commission. In many countries, all individuals or companies that sell tickets are required to be licensed as a travel agent.

In some countries, airlines have stopped giving commissions to travel agencies. Therefore, travel agencies are now forced to charge a percentage premium or a standard flat fee, per sale. However, some companies pay travel agencies a set percentage for selling their product. Major tour companies can afford to do this, because if they were to sell a thousand trips at a cheaper rate, they would still come out better than if they sold a hundred trips at a higher rate. This process benefits both parties. It is also cheaper to offer commissions to travel agents rather than engage in advertising and distribution campaigns without using agents.

Other commercial operations are undertaken, especially by the larger chains. These can include the sale of in-house insurance, travel guide books, and public transport timetables, car rentals, and the services of an on-site bureau de change, dealing in the most popular holiday currencies.

Travel agents in Rio de Janeiro, Brazil.

A travel agent is supposed to offer impartial travel advice to the customer, as well as coordinating travel details and assisting the customer in booking travel. However, this function almost disappeared with the mass market package holiday, and some agency chains seemed to develop a "holiday supermarket" concept, in which customers choose their holiday from brochures on racks and then book it from a counter. Again, a variety of social and economic changes have now contrived to bring this aspect to the fore once more, particularly with the advent of multiple, no-frills, low-cost airlines.

Agency Income

Traditionally, travel agencies' principal source of income was, and continues to be, commissions paid for bookings of car rentals, cruise lines, hotels, railways, sightseeing tours, tour operators, etc. A fixed (in most cases) percentage of the main element of the price is paid to the agent as a commission. Commissions may vary depending on the type of product and the supplier. Commissions are not paid on the tax component of the price. Travel agencies also receive a large variety of bonuses, benefits, and other incentives from travel and tourism related companies as inducements for travel agents to promote their products. The customer is normally not made aware of how much the travel agent is earning in commissions and other benefits. Other sources of income may include the sale of insurance, travel guide books, public transport timetables and money exchange.

Since 1995, many airlines around the world and most airlines in the United States now do not pay any commission to travel agencies. In this case, an agency adds a service fee to the net price. Reduced commissions started in 1995 in the United States, with the introduction of a cap of $50 on return trips and $25 on one way. In 1999, European airlines began eliminating or reducing commissions, while Singapore Airlines did so in parts of Asia. In 2002, Delta Air Lines announced a zero-commission base for the U.S. and Canada; after a few months United Airlines, American Airlines, Continental Airlines, Northwest Airlines, US Airways and American Trans Air all followed suit.

Insurance

The majority of travel agents have felt the need to protect themselves and their clients against the possibilities of commercial failure, either their own or a supplier's. They will advertise the fact that they are surety bonded, meaning in the case of a failure, the customers are guaranteed either an equivalent holiday to that which they have lost or, if they prefer, a refund. Many British and American agencies and tour operators are bonded with the International Air Transport Association (IATA), for those who issue air tickets, Air Travel Organisers' Licensing (ATOL) for those who order tickets in, and the Association of British Travel Agents (ABTA) or the American Society of Travel Agents (ASTA), for those who sell package holidays on behalf of a tour company.

Types of Agencies

There are three different types of agencies in the UK: multiples, miniples, and independent agencies. Multiples comprises a number of national chains, often owned by international conglomerates, like Thomas Cook who are part of the global Thomas Cook Group.It is now common for the large mass market tour companies to purchase a controlling interest in a chain of travel agencies, in order to control the distribution of their product. (This is an example of vertical integration.) The smaller chains are often based in particular regions or districts.

Five different types of agencies exist in the United States: independent, host, franchise,consortium, and mega agencies. American Express and the American Automobile Association (AAA) are examples of mega travel agencies. Carlson Wagonlit Travel is an example of a consortium agency consisting of various types of specialty agencies. An example of an independent travel agency, is one that is started by a sole proprietorship, or partnership between individuals that have no business partnerships with competition agencies. Each type of travel agency has its pros and cons.

Within Australia, many small businesses are sole traders, and often franchisees. They operate online, with a shopfront or as a franchisee. The Australian travel agency industry has increased substantially due to the growth of franchise chains, with small business and sole traders joining franchise networks such as Helloworld Travel, giving them access to internal systems for product and bookings. Flight Centre Travel Group has almost 2,800 company-owned operations and is one of the largest in the world. Booking.com is Australia's most widely used online travel agent.

Independent agencies usually cater to a special or niche market, such as the needs of residents in an upmarket commuter town or suburb, or a particular group interested in a similar activity, such as sporting events, like football, golf, or tennis.

Allamanda Voyages travel agents.

Travel agencies choose between two approaches. One is the traditional, multi-destination, *outbound* travel agency, based in the traveler's originating location; the other is the destination focused, *inbound* travel agency, that is based in the destination and delivers an expertise on that location. At present, the former is usually a larger operator while the latter is often a smaller, independent operator.

Consolidators

Airline consolidators, tour operators, and other types of travel consolidators and wholesalers are high volume sales companies that specialize in selling to niche markets. They may or may not offer various types of services, at a single point of access. These can be hotel reservations, flights or car-rentals. Sometimes the services are combined into vacation packages, that include transfers to the location and lodging. These companies do not usually sell directly to the public, but act as wholesalers to retail travel agencies. Commonly, the sole purpose of consolidators is to sell to ethnic niches in the travel industry. Usually no consolidator offers everything; they may only have contracted rates to specific destinations. Today, there are no domestic consolidators, with some exceptions for business class contracts.

The Difference between Tour Operators and Travel Agents

The main difference is that a tour operator is responsible for operating and providing your vacation through the contracting, booking and packaging together of the various components of your tour such as your hotel, transportation, meals, guides, optional tours and sometimes flight. Many tour operators are considered land only operators and focus on the aspects of your package once you have arrived in your destination.

Travel Agents hold the role of selling and administering packages from various tour operators to their personal clients based on what they're looking for and what package suits each client best. While many tour operators focus on a select concentration of destinations most travel agents can specialize in a range of destinations and then they can help you narrow down a package for that specific destination or area you are looking to travel to based on your budget, preferred method of travel and interests. Travel agents will then work directly with the tour operator to perfect your requests and provide the tour operator with the information and payments they need.

References

- 6-major-components-of-the-tourism-and-travel-industry, knowledge- 111179: shareyouressays.com, Retrieved 08 June, 2019
- Tourism-transportation: tourismnotes.com, Retrieved 28 July, 2019
- The-difference-between-tour-operators-and-travel-agents: tenontours.com, Retrieved 23 March, 2019
- Travel-agency: tourismnotes.com, Retrieved 17 May, 2019
- Pike, Steven; Page, Stephen (2014). "Destination marketing organizations and destination marketing: A narrative analysis of the literature". Tourism Management. 41: 202–207. doi:10.1016/j.tourman.2013.09.009. hdl:2299/20103

7

Tourism: Activities and Accommodations

Activities such as trekking, mountaineering, rafting, paragliding, walking tour, etc. come under tourism activities. Guest ranch, holiday cottage, home exchange, etc. are some examples of tourist accommodations. This chapter closely examines activities and accommodations of tourism to provide an extensive understanding of the subject.

Walking Tour

Walking is one of the purest pleasures of traveling, offering exercise, fresh air and an intimate perspective on the world.

Urban or rural, easy or challenging, guided or independent — somewhere out there is a walking tour to suit your interests and abilities.

Why Walk?

For travelers who are reasonably fit and enjoy being out in the open air, walking trips offer a number of benefits. Traveling on foot is the best way to get a close-up look at a local landscape and culture, whether you're strolling down cobblestone streets or hiking along forest paths. It's the ultimate in slow travel; you'll experience each destination at a leisurely pace, getting within a few yards of the local wildlife and examining the architecture up close rather than whizzing by in a car. As with other forms of slow travel, walking is also a great way to lower your environmental impact.

If you tend to pick up a few pounds on every vacation, a walking tour is the perfect antidote. And unlike other adventure activities such as biking or kayaking, walking is something most travelers can do any time, anywhere, without special training or equipment besides a comfortable pair of shoes.

Why not Walk?

Walking tours are geared toward a variety of fitness levels, but they aren't right for everyone. If you can't walk at a relaxed pace on level ground for at least an hour or two at a time, you may not be physically prepared for a walking tour.

On foot, you may encounter a wide variety of weather conditions, from light rain to extreme heat and humidity. Walking is a more physically demanding experience than riding in a climate-controlled car or bus. Travelers who book a walking tour should be willing to accept some occasional discomfort, including blisters or achy muscles.

Finally, walking is by nature a leisurely style of travel, enabling you to see a limited number of places in an intimate way. Travelers seeking to pack a lot of sightseeing into a small amount of time may be frustrated by the slow pace of a walking trip. If you prefer a faster-paced style of travel, a walking tour may not be right for you.

Walking Tours vs. Traveling Independently

If you want to make walking a major part of your next trip, there are several ways to do it. The easiest way is to book a trip with a tour operator that specializes in walking vacations. (Several are listed below.) They'll plan and guide all of your walks, organize lodging and meals, assist in case of injury, and transport your luggage each day so you don't have to carry it as you walk. Tours are generally led by knowledgeable local guides.

The alternative is to travel independently, either by planning your own walks or by booking individual guided walking tours in each destination that you visit. (Guided walks and city tours are available just about everywhere; to find them, do an Internet search, consult a good guidebook or contact the local tourist office.) Traveling independently allows you a bit more freedom and is usually cheaper than booking a pricey package tour.

Types of Walking Vacations

There are walking vacations to suit nearly every interest and every level of fitness. You can choose an Italian culinary tour that involves easy strolling through small villages, or you can challenge yourself with a week of mountain hiking in the Andes. Accommodations vary widely as well, from camping tents to four-star hotels and luxury inns. Group sizes tend to be on the small size, ranging from 6 to 30 walkers per trip.

The easiest tours blend walking with traditional sightseeing — so you may spend the morning on a country hike and then go shopping, take a cooking class or ride a bus to your next stop in the afternoon. More intense trips may involve walking or hiking steadily throughout the day, or combine walking with other outdoor activities such as kayaking or horseback riding. The most difficult trips are better described as trekking, and typically involve high altitude, rough conditions and specialized equipment. Many companies offer tours in several of these categories, so be sure to read each trip description carefully and choose the appropriate level for you.

Some companies offer special trips for different types of travelers, such as families, women or single travelers. Other tours focus on particular interests, like cooking or history.

Recognizing that some walkers may have different abilities and interests than their traveling companions, some tour operators such as Country Walkers offer multiple options each day — like a moderate hike instead of a difficult one, or a museum visit instead of a walk around the village. Some tours are flexible enough that if you wake up one morning and simply don't feel up to hiking, you won't need to.

Where to Walk

The most popular destinations for walking trips are Europe and the U.S., but you'll also find tours in Canada, New Zealand, Costa Rica, Peru, Morocco, South Africa, China, Southeast Asia and beyond.

How to Prepare

Prepare your body by walking regularly in the weeks before you depart. Try to build up to the kind of walking you'll be doing during your trip, whether that involves hills, long distances or rough terrain. If you'll be carrying a day pack on your trip, bring it along as you train to get used to its weight. Most importantly, wear the same shoes you'll wear for your trip — that way they will be well broken in before the big day.

For more strenuous walking trips, you will want to improve your overall level of fitness in other ways too, such as weight lifting and cardio training.

If you're traveling to a mountainous destination, flying there a day or two early to allow your body to adjust to the altitude. The same goes if you're traveling through many time zones; walking all day is difficult enough on the body without adding jet lag to the mix.

Finally, consider purchasing travel insurance, particularly if you will be hiking in a remote location. This will help protect you in case of injury.

What to Pack for a Walking Vacation

Your tour operator will give you a list of recommended items to pack for your specific itinerary, but here are a few general suggestions:

Comfortable walking shoes — preferably waterproof hiking boots with ankle support (required by some tour operators).

- High-quality, waterproof socks.
- Clothing to suit a variety of weather conditions.
- Day pack.
- Camera.
- Sunscreen.
- Insect repellent.
- Sunglasses.
- Wide-brimmed hat.
- Walking stick or trekking poles for uneven terrain.

Walking Tour Operators

Here are several tour operators offering all-inclusive walking vacations:

- Backroads: Hiking, walking and multi-sport trips in Europe, Latin America, North America, Asia/Pacific and Africa.

- Classic Journeys: Easy-going luxury walking tours in Europe, the Americas, Asia/Pacific, Morocco and Zambia. Trips fall into four categories: cultural walking adventures, culinary tours, family multi-sport trips and private journeys.
- Country Walkers: Both guided and self-guided walking trips, including safaris, around the world.
- Walking Adventures International: Walking tours around the world, which are generally easy to moderate. Not all tours on the company's site are offered in any given year.
- The Wayfarers: Walking vacations in Europe, New Zealand, Argentina and the U.S. Each vacation is rated by activity level, with many easy and moderate options.

Tax-free Shopping

Tax-free shopping (TFS) is the buying of goods in a foreign country and obtaining a refund of the sales tax which has been collected by the retailer on those goods. The sales tax may be variously described as a sales tax, goods and services tax (GST), value added tax (VAT), or consumption tax.

Promoting tax-free shopping and making it easier for tourists to claim the refund back, has helped to attract travellers to many countries. TFS is subject to national regulations, such as minimum spend and restrictions on the types of products on which it can be claimed. Refunds can only be claimed on goods which are exported. However, buying goods tax free does not mean travellers are exempt from paying applicable taxes on their purchases when they get home.

Tax-free Shopping Countries

Fifty-five of the 130 countries that levy VAT/GST allow foreign visitors to have their taxes reimbursed.

Tax-free shopping is currently available in the following countries: Argentina, Armenia, Australia, Austria, Azerbaijan, Belgium, Bulgaria, Canada, Croatia, Cyprus, Czech Republic, Denmark,

Estonia, Finland, France, Germany, Greece, Hungary, Iceland, Indonesia, Ireland, Israel, Italy, Japan, Korea, Latvia, Lebanon, Liechtenstein, Lithuania, Luxembourg, Macedonia, Malaysia, Mexico, Morocco, the Netherlands, Norway, Poland, Portugal, Romania, Russia, Serbia, Singapore, Slovenia, Slovakia, Spain, South Africa, Sweden, Switzerland, Taiwan, Thailand, Turkey, the United Kingdom, the United States and Vietnam.

Travellers resident in a country outside the EU, can shop tax-free at shops outside EU airports. The traveller pays the VAT over goods in the shop and can request a refund when leaving the European Union with the goods. General restrictions are that a traveller must be a resident in a non-EU country, has a maximum stay of 6 months when visiting the EU, purchases are made up to three months prior to export, and only goods meant for personal use are eligible for the refund. Travellers need to keep the purchase receipts and visit Customs before leaving the EU to get an export validation stamp. Receipts can then be sent back to the retailers for a refund request.

Each country in the EU has a different VAT rate which is reclaimable, and most have a minimum purchase amount restriction however there are exceptions. For example, in July 2018 the minimum spend limit of €90.16 was lifted in Spain. Tax free shopping is now a benefit which can be enjoyed by all non EU residents visiting Spain, and no longer just for affluent travel shoppers, purchasing luxury goods. Furthermore, in January 2019 it became compulsory for all retailers to support travel shoppers in the process of reclaiming VAT refunds. This initiative has been introduced by the Spanish government to boost the travel and retail sectors. There is now an added emphasis on retailers to work with tax-free operators to educate international shoppers on the benefit whilst supporting them in reclaiming their tax refunds.

VAT Rates and Minimum Purchases Required to Qualify for Refunds Country of Purchase VAT Standard Rate* Minimum in Local Currency Austria 20% €75.01 Belgium 21% €50 Bulgaria 20% 250 BGN Croatia 25% 740 HRK Czech Republic 21% 2,001 CZK Denmark 25% 300 DKK Estonia 20% €38.01 Finland 24% €40 France 20% €175.01 Germany 19% €25 Great Britain 20% £30 Greece 24% €50 Hungary 27% 54,001 HUF Iceland 24% 6,000 ISK Ireland 23% €30 Italy 22% €155 Latvia 21% €44 Lithuania 21% €55 Luxembourg 17% €74 Malta 18% €100 Netherlands 21% €50 Norway 25% 315 NOK Poland 23% 200 PLN Portugal 23% €61.35 Romania 19% 250 RON Slovakia 20% €100 Slovenia 22% €50.01 Spain 21% €90.16 Sweden 25% 200 SEK Switzerland 8% 300 CHF Turkey 18% 118 TRY.

Some jurisdictions in the United States allow a refund of sales tax to foreign tourists upon leaving the country.

Tax-free shopping is a privilege enjoyed by all residents of United States jurisdictions without sales taxes, but through so-called "remote" sales — including sales to visiting out-of-state residents, sales via catalog, and sales via Internet — customers in a sales taxed jurisdiction may also make purchases in sales tax-free jurisdictions, notwithstanding the legal requirement to pay the equivalent (compensatory) use tax in their home state. Delaware is free of all sales taxes, excluding homes and cars (3% transfer tax for real estate, and a 2.75% tag fee for cars). The Christiana Mall near Newark, Delaware attracts shoppers from the nearby states of Maryland, New Jersey, New York, and Pennsylvania looking to save money on purchases from not having to pay sales tax. The Apple Store at the Christiana Mall claims to sell more iPhones than any other location in the chain due to Delaware's lack of sales tax. Merchants in tax-free New Hampshire regularly advertise to residents of adjacent Massachusetts, Vermont, and Maine the benefits of purchasing goods without sales tax, ignoring the fact that there is no general exemption from the use taxes when the goods are taken back home. Many purchasers are unaware of the obligation to pay the tax, or file the necessary return, or of the fact that it is not the duty of a merchant to collect it from them and pay it indirectly. However, it is the purchaser's obligation to pay it directly to the state, often in connection with filing their annual income tax return.

The liability of any non-exempt resident of a US state with a sales tax for payment of the equivalent use tax when purchasing goods from another state (or country) through mail-order, by telephone or through the Internet should not be confused with the issue of direct Internet taxes levied on Internet services themselves, such as bit taxes, bandwidth taxes, franchise taxes, and email taxes. Most such levies are banned until 2014 by the Internet Tax Freedom Act Amendment Acts of 2007 which extends the provisions in the federal Internet Tax Freedom Act beyond its original 2007 expiration.

Goods that would be taxable at home are taxable at the same rate when taken home or delivered, regardless of where or how they were purchased. Numerous local sales tax and use tax exemptions exist according to taxpayer status (for example, there exist exemptions for charitable organizations), exemptions based on size of purchase (e.g., clothing under $110 in Vermont), and exemptions for specific types of goods (e.g., protective clothing, food, medication, and educational materials).

Even customers from jurisdictions that levy sales taxes can in theory have additional tax liabilities when shopping in neighboring no-tax or lower-tax jurisdictions. For example, if an adjacent state has a slightly lower tax rate than the purchaser's home, that shopper could face an additional tax burden even though the purchase was already taxed at the point of sale. The difference in tax rates is referred to by collecting authorities as "tax discount".

Taxing jurisdictions generally extend an exemption from use tax to commercial taxpayers that purchase business stock. This type of exemption applies to goods purchased tax-free for resale, but lapses if the goods are converted to use by the company itself (for example, a company car, office supplies, and cleaning supplies).

Some countries charge a value added tax (VAT) or goods and services tax (GST) that extends to retail purchases. When those customers are residents of a US state having sales taxes on such goods, the VAT or GST taxes paid might be used as a credit against the amount of use tax otherwise owed, unless excluded, such as in Massachusetts. However, when a post-travel refund of the VAT or GST is claimed, the purchaser's home taxing jurisdiction can then assert a claim for the full sales tax liability.

Despite the fact that most shoppers are unaware of their use tax obligations, there are potentially severe penalties for willful tax evasion. Any online, telephone mail-order, or traveling shopper who makes "tax free" purchases could be successfully prosecuted for evading state use taxes if he or she willfully fails to file the necessary return and pay the required tax, or intentionally omits the information from a required annual return. When a taxing jurisdiction enforces use tax liability, it often also seeks additional penalties and interest accrued for failure to timely remit the necessary tax return and tax payments, as well as possible perjury for omissions on official forms filed. The statute of limitations on taxes due may not begin to run until and unless a required tax return is filed. Some states also provide a "safe harbor" scale of use tax that is most likely owed by every taxpayer, based upon the taxpayer's adjusted gross income. For example, someone with an income of over $100,000 could earmark 0.0005 of his or income as payment for "use tax", without having to account for any actual out-of-state purchases under $1,000 each.

To step up the opportunity for collection of use taxes, several US states have been working to implement a "streamlined" interstate use tax agreement. To effectuate this multilateral interstate compact, many states have enacted, or are considering enacting, statutory changes that require residents to disclose, under penalty of perjury, their annual use tax liability for out-of-state purchases. The focus on use tax collection has increased because the U.S. Supreme Court has placed significant hurdles in the path of state efforts to collect sales taxes on transactions in other no-tax or lower-tax jurisdictions. In *National Bellas Hess, Inc. v. Department of Revenue of the State of Illinois* and *Quill Corp. v. North Dakota*, the Court concluded that the Commerce Clause and Due Process Clause of the U.S. Constitution require that there be a nexus between the taxing state and the vendor of goods or services, in the form of a physical presence. This has been interpreted to apply to both catalog sales and out of state sales over the Internet. States are thus prohibited from collecting sales taxes on so-called remote transactions because to do so would unconstitutionally burden interstate commerce. The Streamlined sales tax project is the states' response, by which they are seeking to collect use taxes on remote Internet and catalog sales in lieu of sales taxes.

In connection with the Streamlined sales tax project there has been discussion among state tax officials of creating obligations or incentives for merchants to collect taxes from customers who are residents of sales tax states, especially in the area of online sales, in exchange for a remitting to the merchant a percentage of the taxes that would be otherwise unpaid. Some US states are also considering a tax amnesty, pursuant to which residents could settle unpaid use taxes and penalties at a discount, but only if the settlement is offered before collection of the tax liability commences.

In Australia tax-free shopping is called the Tourist Refund Scheme (TRS) which allows overseas visitors and Australian residents to claim a refund of the Goods and Services Tax (GST) and Wine equalisation tax (WET) paid on certain goods bought in Australia within 60 days of leaving Australia, and then taken out of Australia in carry-on bags or worn. The refund is available on goods purchased in the 60 days before leaving Australia, purchases from any single business (even on separate invoices) must total $300 (GST inclusive) or more, the traveller must have an original tax invoice for the goods, the goods may require to be verified by an officer at the Customs and Border Protection Client Services counter.

Claims for a tax refund can be made at the TRS counter in an international airport or the cruiseliner terminal of some Australian seaports.

Refund

The refunded amount corresponds to the VAT or GST paid and in which country the traveller buys goods. VAT/GST is a tax added to the cost of a product, calculated as a percentage of the products retail price. Often in Europe, the ticket price includes VAT, this is less often the case in the US. As an example, if the VAT rate on a product is 20% and the ticket price is displayed as €100, including VAT, the VAT will be €16.67 (83.33 + 20% VAT = €100.).

A handling fee may be charged by the service provider.

Tourist Accommodation

Accommodation is one of the basic needs for any tourism activity. Travelers and tourists need lodging for rest, while they are on a tour. Accommodation in the form of low budget lodges/hotels to world class luxury hotels is available at all the major tourist destinations to provide the tourist a home away from home. These are establishments that provide a place for the tourist to stay i.e. lodging facilities which are paid for the duration of the stay by the tourist. There are various types of accommodation which are being used by tourists regularly. Travel agents and tour operators generally include one of the following types of accommodation in the itinerary.

Hotel

Hotels are a vital and essential part of the tourism industry. Today, hotels not only provide accommodation and meals but also offer a variety of other services as per the needs of the tourist/ guest. For example, many hotels offer a health club, crèche, etc. as per the changing needs of the customer.

International or Star Category Hotel

They are the modern western style hotels, found mostly in metro cities and at major tourist destinations and that are located at prime locations in the city. These hotels are classified on the internationally accepted star grading which ranges from five stars to one star. The grading is given to the hotel depending on the facilities and services which the hotel provides. The facilities which are provided by the five star are an information desk, conference centre, travel desk, multi cuisine restaurants, banquet halls, room service, swimming pool, gymnasium, health clubs, shopping arcades, beauty parlours, entertainment or cultural programmes, etc.

Motels

They are located on highways and expressways. The tourists who are on transient mode and cost conscious prefer to stay in these kinds of accommodation. These motels not only provide parking space but also certain amenities such as television, restaurants swimming pool, etc.

Non Star or Commercial Hotels

These hotels are located mostly near the business or commercial centres and mainly serve the business tourists, middle income tourists and their repeat customers. Most of these hotels are equipped with parking space, restaurants, and facilities for their business clients/guests such as convention centers and meeting rooms.

Floating Hotels

These types of hotels are located on the surface of the water which may be the sea, river, or lake water. These hotels have facilities which are similar to a regular hotel. Examples: House boats of Kashmir and Kerala or old cruise liners which have been converted into a hotel.

Capsule Hotels

These were first opened in Osaka, Japan in 1979. These hotels serve mostly the business tourists. The rooms in the capsule are lined similar to that of a 'double-decker', or sleeping compartment of a AC 2 tier train. Common washrooms, vending machines, and a lounge area are located on each floor. Facilities such as a bed, a television, flexible lighting, a box for valuables, etc. are provided in each capsule rooms.

Heritage Hotels

These are the old properties like castles, forts, palaces, and havelis belonging to royalty which have been renovated and converted into hotels. Here, tourists enjoy the majestic grandeur and splendor of the olden days.

Resorts

These cater to the tourists who look for rest, relaxation and recreation. They are located mostly at the sea side, hill stations, wild life sanctuaries, etc. Apart from facilities provided by hotels, resorts provide additional facilities to guest for recreation and relaxation which includes indoor and out door games, gambling, spa, etc.

Guest Ranch

A guest ranch, also known as a dude ranch, is a type of ranch oriented towards visitors or tourism. It is considered a form of agritourism.

Guest ranches arose in response to the romanticization of the American West that began to occur in the late 19th century. In 1893, historian Frederick Jackson Turner stated that the United States frontier was demographically "closed". This in turn led many people to have feelings of nostalgia for bygone days, but also, given that the risks of a true frontier were gone, allowed for nostalgia to be indulged in relative safety. Thus, the person referred to as a "tenderfoot" or a "greenhorn" by westerners was finally able to visit and enjoy the advantages of western life for a short period of time without needing to risk life and limb.

The Western adventures of famous figures, like Theodore Roosevelt, were made available to paying guests from cities of the East, called "dudes" in the West. In the early years, the transcontinental railroad network brought paying visitors to a local depot, where a wagon or buggy would be waiting to transport people to a ranch. Experiences varied. Some guest ranch visitors expected a somewhat edited and more luxurious version of the "cowboy life", while others were more tolerant of the odors and timetable of a working ranch. While there were guest ranches prior to the 20th century, the trend grew considerably after the end of World War I, when postwar prosperity, the invention of the automobile and the appearance of Western movies all increased popular interest in the west. In 1926 the Dude Ranchers Association was founded in Cody, Wyoming, to represent the needs of this rapidly growing industry.

In the US, guest ranches are now a long-established tradition and continue to be a vacation destination. Depending on the climate, some guest ranches are open only in the summer or winter, while others offer year-round service. Some of the activities offered at many guest ranches include horseback riding, target shooting, cattle sorting, hayrides, campfire sing-alongs, hiking, camping, whitewater rafting, zip-lining, archery and fishing. College students are often recruited to work at guest ranches during the summer months. Common jobs offered to college students include: housekeeping, wrangler, dining staff, and office staff or babysitters. A number of working ranches have survived lean financial times by taking in paying guests for part of the year.

Hunting Ranches

Some guest ranches cater to hunters. Some feature native wildlife such as whitetail deer, mule deer, bison or elk. Others feature exotic species imported from other regions and nations such as Africa and India. Both types of ranches are controversial. While many traditional ranches allow hunters and outfitters on their land to hunt native game, the act of confining game to guarantee a kill is considered unsporting by some.

The introduction of non-native species on ranches is more controversial because of concerns that these "exotics" may escape and contaminate the gene pool of native species, or spread previously unknown diseases. The advocates of hunting ranches argue in turn that they help protect native herds from over-hunting, and that the stocking of exotic species actually increases their numbers and may help save them from extinction.

Holiday Cottage

A holiday cottage, holiday home, or vacation property is accommodation used for holiday vacations, corporate travel, and temporary housing often for less than 30 days. Such properties are typically small homes, such as cottages, that travelers can rent and enjoy as if it were their own home for the duration of their stay. The properties may be owned by those using them for a vacation, in which case the term second home applies; or may be rented out to holidaymakers through an agency.

Holiday cottages in converted farm buildings.

Purpose-built holiday cottages.

Terminology varies among countries. In the United Kingdom this type of property is usually termed a *holiday home* or *holiday cottage*; in Australia, a *holiday house/home*, or *weekender*; in New Zealand, a *bach* or *crib*.

Seventies architecture.

Characteristics and Advantages

A second home or vacation home can be a home owner's asset as renting it could provide additional income. Vacationers are opting for a single family residence that they can rent on a nightly or weekly basis. Vacation type properties are becoming popular not only for existing homes but also for building one.

Holiday cottages are found across the UK, with many destinations from town houses to forests. Many areas in the UK have seen a growth in the Holiday Cottage industry such as the Lake District and Cornwall. There are typically two routes to renting a holiday cottage. Either direct with an owner, or through the auspices of a holiday cottage agency. Several holiday home portals list cottages available direct from the owner, and charge an fee for listing the property.

Today's global short-term vacation property rental market is estimated to be worth $100 billion. The holiday cottage market in both Canada and the UK is highly competitive – and big business. In the UK, this increased competition has led to significant improvements in the quality of properties on offer. This improvement in standards has in turn contributed to the increase in the popularity of holiday cottages for weekend breaks, offering in many cases the same standard of accommodation as an hotel, yet with the increased freedom that a holiday cottage offers.

One other significant development in the UK holiday cottage market is that of Farm Stays, driven partly by the farmers and the returns they get from farming itself, but also by the desire of parents wanting their children to experience rural life first-hand.

The rapid development of the Internet and technologies such as telephony and personal digital assistants that allow people to work from home since circa 1995 has blurred the division between vacation property and a primary residence. Some business people, including the British entrepreneur Richard Branson, use their luxury real estate for both business and leisure purposes.

Costs and Effects

Financial and Legal Implications

In the UK, furnished holiday lettings offer other tax relief providing certain conditions are met. The current conditions are:

- It should be available for commercial letting to the public for a total of 140 days in the 12-month period.
- It must be let for at least 70 days in the 12-month period. (Where more than one qualifying property is held, it is possible to average the number of days all properties are let in total in order to meet this condition).
- The total periods of long term occupation may not exceed 155 days during the 12-month period.

Second home and holiday home owners used to be able to claim discounts in their council tax in the United Kingdom, as the property is vacant for much of the year. This is no longer true in many areas, including Carmarthenshire; if the property is empty (but furnished) no discount is permitted and the owner will be liable to pay the tax in full. But, In Cornwall, since 2004 second home owners can claim a 10% discount in their council tax. Prior to 2004, they could claim a 50% discount in Cornwall, they are still able to claim 50% in many other areas in England. The Welsh movement, Cymuned, promote the principle that owners of holiday homes should pay double the standard rate of council tax, as they do not otherwise invest in the local community. Testimony of this is to be seen in a report on the effect of holiday homes in Scotland, which found that those who went on holiday to Scotland spent an average of £57 a day, in comparison to just £32 a day spent by those visiting their holiday or second homes.

Community

Owners of holiday homes will occasionally move to their second homes permanently upon retirement, this can be a threat to the culture of an area, especially in Wales where the influx of non-Welsh speakers affects the percentage of Welsh speakers in the area and reduces the use of Welsh in everyday life. Hundreds of second homes were burnt between 1979 and the mid-1990s as a part of a campaign by nationalist movement Meibion Glyndŵr to protect the indigenous language and culture.

Home Exchange

Home swaps usually occur simultaneously. For instance, imagine you live in New York and want to visit Paris for a week. First, you'd find someone in Paris who wishes to visit New York. Then, both of you would vacation at the same time and stay in each other's home during the same week.

However, if you'll be away on business or a separate vacation while they wish to visit, you can still swap out your home. In this case, you simply arrange to stay at their home at a later date.

Hosting an Exchange

Some home exchange sites allow you to "host" your exchanger. This is called a hospitality exchange. You can go this route if your vacation times don't match up or if you simply like the idea of hosting.

Basically, you stay at home while your exchanger visits one week, and then you visit them a different week. Swapping homes while you're still at home allows you to develop friendships with your exchange family and get an inside look at who they are.

Benefits of Home Swapping

The benefits of home swapping are many and make for a unique vacation experience that isn't available via traditional lodging options.

It is Low-cost

When you swap homes, you don't pay a dime for your lodging. The only cost associated with house swapping is the membership fee for the online listing service (which is essential to find someone to swap with). These fees are usually $100 or more per year, but since the average price for one night in a hotel often exceeds $100, most people find this to be a bargain.

Another travel expense that can get prohibitive is eating out. But since you'll have a full kitchen to cook in, you won't need to eat three meals "out" every day. Plus, you'll get to experience local grocery shopping, which can be quite different in other countries. Further, if you and your host agree to swap cars, you'll eliminate car rental costs as well.

Live like a Local

Staying in someone's home rather than a hotel is often more comfortable; there are usually movies to watch, books to read, and perhaps even toys for your kids to play with. Some homes have a pool or fitness room as well. Remember, when you swap, you're in an actual home and not an impersonal hotel room.

You're also more likely to get a better sense of the area's culture because you're in a neighborhood rather than a hotel. Living amidst "the locals" can add a depth of perspective to your trip that you would otherwise miss out on in a hotel or tourist-centric area.

Utilize your Second Home

Home exchange is especially easy if you have a vacation home. Because you're not living there year round, you don't have to try as hard to coordinate schedules. You can make your home available to a wider array of exchangers with different travel needs.

Want to Stay on a Yacht?

Home exchanges don't always involve homes. People swap homes to stay in someone's yacht, or even their RV so they can tour an area. You can often find unique lodging options that are unavailable, or quite expensive, via other means.

Downsides of Home Swapping

As with virtually everything else, there are cons as well as pros to swapping houses. Here are a few to consider:

Strangers Living in each other's Homes

Some people are uncomfortable with the idea of a complete stranger staying in their home. This is why it's so important to use a reputable listing service. These services give you a detailed look at a potential exchanger's home online (and they get a detailed look at yours).

That said, because you live in different locales, your interaction is obviously limited. You may not feel able to gather enough information to assess whether or not a potential exchanger is worthy of your home. This is one reason why some people "host" their exchanger the first time around.

Potential Damage to Property

You might also be concerned about your valuables, or that your property or items might be damaged by strangers. Again, this is why using a reputable listing service is essential. The biggest sites report that they have never had a complaint from any user because of theft or vandalism.

On the whole, house swappers are considerate and educated people. They will likely treat your home, and your possessions, with as much respect as they treat their own. Remember, you will be occupying their house as well and they are probably concerned about the same things you are. Also, it does not hurt to make sure your insurance covers your valuables in an amount that is equal to or exceeds their worth.

Time Investment

Home exchanges take time to set up. You cannot and would not want to just book your desired dates. Remember, you need to get to know the people you will be exchanging with, and vice versa. In fact, most sites recommend starting your search at least four to six months before you plan to go on vacation. You will also want to be flexible on the exact location and dates.

8

Technological Aspects of Tourism

There are a number of technological provisions that aid tourists. Electronic ticket, flight tracking, biometric passport, online hotel reservations, mobile ticketing, audio tour, virtual tour, global distribution system are some of the provisions that fall in this domain. All these diverse technological aspects of tourism have been carefully analyzed in this chapter.

Electronic Ticket

An e-ticket carries the same information as a paper ticket. The major difference is an e-ticket is located in an airline's computer database, instead of the passenger's suitcase. It is an electronic record of the traveler's airline reservation, containing information such as the time, date and place of the flight, airport, seat assignment and travel class. At the gate, e-ticket passengers need only show a valid photo identification card such as a driver's license to claim their spot on the aircraft. Once the airline confirms the traveler's information, it issues a boarding pass that the traveler uses to board the plane.

Traditional travel companies, such as airlines or travel agencies, can assist travelers with obtaining e-tickets. But improving Internet technology also allows passengers to book their flights on their own. In fact, the passenger who uses this self-serve option may not even come into contact with the airline until arriving at the airport and presenting his ID.

To issue e-tickets, airlines must have a database that is integrated with an airline's passenger service system. That is then connected to all other partners airlines, airports, ground transportation and travel agencies, for instance to share real time information.

To book themselves on a flight, travelers can visit any number of Web-based ticketing sites. Once there, they can view the options available and use a credit or debit card to pay for their ticket. After placing the order, the electronic record of the ticket goes into the airline's database, where it holds the passenger's spot.

E-tickets have virtually replaced traditional paper tickets in the majority of airports and airlines around the world.

Flight Tracking

The Flight Tracker service provides notification every time there is a significant update in the flight status.

Flight Tracking is an activity by enthusiasts or concerned citizens. Tracking is not limited to aircraft activity; it can also include airport activity. Flight tracking via software is a relatively new activity.

Flight/airline tracking, that is the use of flight trackers has been growing due to the obvious reason to know whether a flight has safely landed or whether everything goes according to the schedule so it is the time to go to the airport.

With development of cell phones and other small PDA devices, flight trackers have become a must-have for people who are concerned about arrivals and departures of airplanes. Modern trackers can track airlines virtually all around the world and inform concerned parties via such commonplace mediums as SMS. The integration of flight tracking into travel management and travel tracking services is a new frontier, allowing increased automation of travel software. This application of flight tracking is currently in its infancy, but is set to grow significantly as systems get more connected.

Despite all the progress, many abrupt events like sudden weather changes are not captured by existing flight trackers because they take their information not from the airplane itself but from dispatcher centers which often do not know the actual status of plane's whereabouts.

Flight tracking software is available for commercial operators to track their aircraft and monitor if they deviate from the agreed flight path, if so, a warning alarm is generated to alert to a potential problem. The type of software available also imports and reviews global weather and NOTAM information to monitor any emerging issues that could affect the flight.

Biometric Passport

A biometric passport (also known as an e-passport, ePassport, or a digital passport) is a traditional passport that has an embedded electronic microprocessor chip which contains biometric information that can be used to authenticate the identity of the passport holder. It uses contactless smart card technology, including a microprocessor chip (computer chip) and antenna (for both power to the chip and communication) embedded in the front or back cover, or centre page, of the passport. The passport's critical information is printed on the data page of the passport, repeated on the machine readable lines and stored in the chip. Public key infrastructure (PKI) is used to authenticate the data stored electronically in the passport chip, making it expensive and difficult to forge when all security mechanisms are fully and correctly implemented.

Many countries are moving towards the issue of biometric passports. Malaysia was the first country to issue biometric passports in 1998. In December 2008, 60 countries were issuing such passports, which increased to 120 by June 2017.

This biometric symbol is usually printed on the cover of biometric passports.

The currently standardised biometrics used for this type of identification system are facial recognition, fingerprint recognition, and iris recognition. These were adopted after assessment of several different kinds of biometrics including retinal scan. Document and chip characteristics are documented in the International Civil Aviation Organization's (ICAO) Doc 9303 (ICAO9303). The ICAO defines the biometric file formats and communication protocols to be used in passports. Only the digital image (usually in JPEG or JPEG2000 format) of each biometric feature is actually stored in the chip. The comparison of biometric features is performed outside the passport chip by electronic border control systems (e-borders). To store biometric data on the contactless chip, it includes a minimum of 32 kilobytes of EEPROM storage memory, and runs on an interface in accordance with the ISO/IEC 14443 international standard, amongst others. These standards intend interoperability between different countries and different manufacturers of passport books.

Some national identity cards, such as those from the Netherlands, Albania and Brazil), are fully ICAO9303 compliant biometric travel documents. However others, such as the United States Passport Card, are not.

Data Protection

Biometric passports have protection mechanisms to avoid and/or detect attacks:

- Non-traceable chip characteristics:

  Random chip identifiers reply to each request with a different chip number. This prevents tracing of passport chips. Using random identification numbers is optional.

- Basic Access Control (BAC):

  BAC protects the communication channel between the chip and the reader by encrypting transmitted information. Before data can be read from a chip, the reader needs to provide a key which is derived from the Machine Readable Zone: the date of birth, the date of expiry and the document number. If BAC is used, an attacker cannot (easily) eavesdrop transferred information without knowing the correct key. Using BAC is optional.

- Passive Authentication (PA):

  PA is aimed at identifying modification of passport chip data. The chip contains a file, Document Security Object (SOD), that stores hash values of all files stored in the chip (picture, fingerprint, etc.) and a digital signature of these hashes. The digital signature is made using a document signing key which itself is signed by a country signing key. If a file in the chip (e.g., the picture) is changed, this can be detected since the hash value is incorrect. Readers need access to all used public country keys to check whether the digital signature is generated by a trusted country. Using PA is mandatory. According to a September 2011 United States Central Intelligence Agency document released by "Although falsified e-passports will not have the correct digital signature, inspectors may not detect the fraud if the passports are from countries that do not participate in the International Civil Aviation Organization's Public Key Directory (ICAO PKD).

- Active Authentication (AA):

  AA prevents cloning of passport chips. The chip contains a private key that cannot be read or copied, but its existence can easily be proven. Using AA is optional.

- Extended Access Control (EAC):

  EAC adds functionality to check the authenticity of both the chip (chip authentication) and the reader (terminal authentication). Furthermore, it uses stronger encryption than BAC. EAC is typically used to protect fingerprints and iris scans. Using EAC is optional. In the European Union, using EAC is mandatory for all documents issued starting 28 June 2009.

- Supplemental Access Control (SAC):

  SAC was introduced by ICAO in 2009 for addressing BAC weaknesses. It was introduced as a supplement to BAC (for keeping compatibility), but will replace it in the future.

- Shielding the chip:

  This prevents unauthorised reading. Some countries – including at least the US – have integrated a very thin metal mesh into the passport's cover to act as a shield when the passport cover is closed. The use of shielding is optional.

To assure interoperability and functionality of the security mechanisms listed above, ICAO and German Federal Office for Information Security (BSI) have specified several test cases. These test specifications are updated with every new protocol and are covering details starting from the paper used and ending in the chip that is included.

Attacks

Since the introduction of biometric passports, several attacks have been presented and demonstrated.

- Non-traceable chip characteristics:

  In 2008 a Radboud/Lausitz University team demonstrated that it's possible to determine which country a passport chip is from without knowing the key required for reading it. The team fingerprinted error messages of passport chips from different countries. The resulting lookup table allows an attacker to determine from where a chip originated. In 2010 Tom Chothia and Vitaliy Smirnov documented an attack that allows an individual passport to be traced, by sending specific BAC authentication requests. In 2016 Avoine et al. published a survey on security and privacy issues in passport protocols, where a new technique to track passports is introduced, based on the response time of basic commands.

- Basic Access Control (BAC):

  In 2005 Marc Witteman showed that the document numbers of Dutch passports were predictable, allowing an attacker to guess/crack the key required for reading the chip. In 2006 Adam Laurie wrote software that tries all known passport keys within a given range, thus implementing one of Witteman's attacks. Using online flight booking sites, flight coupons and other public information it's possible to significantly reduce the number of possible keys. Laurie demonstrated the attack by reading the chip of a *Daily Mail* reporter's passport in its envelope without opening it. Note that in some early biometric passports BAC wasn't used at all, allowing attacker to read the chip's content without providing a key.

- Passive Authentication (PA):

  In 2006 Lukas Grunwald demonstrated that it is trivial to copy passport data from a passport chip into a standard ISO/IEC 14443 smartcard using a standard contactless card interface and a simple file transfer tool. Grunwald used a passport that did not use Active Authentication (anti-cloning) and did not change the data held on the copied chip, thus keeping its cryptographic signature valid.

  In 2008 Jeroen van Beek demonstrated that not all passport inspection systems check the cryptographic signature of a passport chip. For his demonstration Van Beek altered chip information and signed it using his own document signing key of a non-existing country. This can only be detected by checking the country signing keys that are used to sign the document signing keys. To check country signing keys the ICAO PKD can be used. Only 5 out of 60+ countries are using this central database. Van Beek did not update the original passport chip: instead an ePassport emulator was used.

  Also in 2008, The Hacker's Choice implemented all attacks and published code to verify the results. The release included a video clip that demonstrated problems by using a forged Elvis Presley passport that is recognized as a valid US passport.

- Active Authentication (AA):

  In 2005 Marc Witteman showed that the secret Active Authentication key can be retrieved using power analysis. This may allow an attacker to clone passport chips that use the optional Active Authentication anti-cloning mechanism on chips – if the chip design is susceptible to this attack.

  In 2008 Jeroen van Beek demonstrated that optional security mechanisms can be disabled by removing their presence from the passport index file. This allows an attacker to remove – amongst others – anti-cloning mechanisms (Active Authentication). The attack is documented in supplement 7 of Doc 9303 (R1-p1_v2_sIV_0006) and can be solved by patching inspection system software. Note that supplement 7 features vulnerable examples in the same document that – when implemented – result in a vulnerable inspection process.

- Extended Access Control (EAC):

  In 2007 Lukas Grunwald presented an attack that can make EAC-enabled passport chips unusable. Grunwald states that if an EAC-key – required for reading fingerprints and updating certificates – is stolen or compromised, an attacker can upload a false certificate with an issue date far in the future. The affected chips block read access until the future date is reached.

Opposition

Privacy proponents in many countries question and protest the lack of information about exactly what the passports' chip will contain, and whether they impact civil liberties. The main problem they point out is that data on the passports can be transferred with wireless RFID technology, which can become a major vulnerability. Although this could allow ID-check computers to obtain a person's information without a physical connection, it may also allow anyone with the necessary equipment to perform the same task. If the personal information and passport numbers on the chip are not encrypted, the information might wind up in the wrong hands.

The BBC published an article on the British ePassport, citing the above stories and adding that:

> Nearly every country issuing this passport has a few security experts who are yelling at the top of their lungs and trying to shout out: 'This is not secure. This is not a good idea to use this technology'", citing a specialist who states "It is much too complicated. It is in places done the wrong way round – reading data first, parsing data, interpreting data, then verifying whether it is right. There are lots of technical flaws in it and there are things that have just been forgotten, so it is basically not doing what it is supposed to do. It is supposed to get a higher security level. It is not.

The Future of Identity in the Information Society (FIDIS) network's research team (a body of IT security experts funded by the European Union) has "also come out against the ePassport scheme. European governments have forced a document on its people that dramatically decreases security and increases the risk of identity theft."

Most security measures are designed against untrusted citizens (the "provers"), but the scientific security community recently also addressed the threats from untrustworthy verifiers, such as corrupt governmental organizations, or nations using poorly implemented, unsecure electronic systems. New cryptographic solutions such as private biometrics are being proposed to mitigate threats of mass theft of identity. These are under scientific study, but not yet implemented in biometric passports.

Computer Reservation System

Computer reservation systems, or central reservation systems (CRS), are computerized systems used to store and retrieve information and conduct transactions related to air travel, hotels, car rental, or other activities. Originally designed and operated by airlines, CRSs were later extended for use by travel agencies. global distribution systems (GDS) to book and sell tickets for multiple airlines. Most airlines have outsourced their CRSs to GDS companies, which also enable consumer access through Internet gateways. Modern GDSs typically also allow users to book hotel rooms, rental cars, airline tickets as well as other activities and tours. They also provide access to railway reservations and bus reservations in some markets, although these are not always integrated with the main system. These are also used to relay computerized information for users in the hotel industry, making reservation and ensuring that the hotel is not overbooked.

Airline reservations systems may be integrated into a larger passenger service system, which also includes an airline inventory system and a departure control system.

In 1946, American Airlines installed the first automated booking system, the experimental electro-mechanical Reservisor. A newer machine with temporary storage based on a magnetic drum, the Magnetronic Reservisor, soon followed. This system proved successful, and was soon being used by several airlines, as well as Sheraton Hotels and Goodyear for inventory control. It was seriously hampered by the need for local human operators to do the actual lookups; ticketing agents would have to call a booking office, whose operators would direct a small team operating the Reservisor and then read the results over the telephone. There was no way for agents to directly query the system.

The MARS-1 train ticket reservation system was designed and planned in the 1950s by the Japanese National Railways' R&D Institute, now the Railway Technical Research Institute, with the system eventually being produced by Hitachi in 1958. It was the world's first seat reservation system for trains. The MARS-1 was capable of reserving seat positions, and was controlled by a transistor computer with a central processing unit and a 400,000-bit magnetic drum memory unit to hold seating files. It used many registers, to indicate whether seats in a train were vacant or reserved to accelerate searches of and updates to seat patterns, for communications with terminals, printing reservation notices, and CRT displays.

Remote Access

In 1953, Trans-Canada Airlines (TCA) started investigating a computer-based system with remote terminals, testing one design on the University of Toronto's Manchester Mark 1 machine that summer. Though successful, the researchers found that input and output was a major problem. Ferranti Canada became involved in the project and suggested a new system using punched cards and a transistorized computer in place of the unreliable tube-based Mark I. The resulting system, ReserVec, started operation in 1962, and took over all booking operations in January 1963. Terminals were placed in all of TCA's ticketing offices, allowing all queries and bookings to complete in about one second with no remote operators needed.

In 1953, American Airlines CEO C. R. Smith chanced to sit next to R. Blair Smith, a senior IBM sales representative, on a flight from Los Angeles to New York. C.R. invited Blair to visit their Reservisor system and look for ways that IBM could improve the system. Blair alerted Thomas Watson Jr. that American was interested in a major collaboration, and a series of low-level studies started. Their idea of an automated airline reservation system (ARS) resulted in a 1959 venture known as the Semi-Automatic Business Research Environment (SABRE), launched the following year. By the time the network was completed in December 1964, it was the largest civil data processing system in the world.

Other airlines established their own systems. Pan American World Airways launched its PANAMAC system in 1964. Delta Air Lines launched the Delta Automated Travel Account System (DATAS) in 1968. United Airlines and Trans World Airlines followed in 1971 with the Apollo Reservation System and Programmed Airline Reservation System (PARS), respectively. Soon, travel agents began pushing for a system that could automate their side of the process by accessing the various ARSes directly to make reservations. Fearful this would place too much power in the hands of agents, American Airlines executive Robert Crandall proposed creating an industry-wide computer reservation system to be a central clearing house for U.S. travel; other airlines demurred, citing fear of antitrust prosecution.

Travel Agent Access

In 1976, United began offering its Apollo system to travel agents; while it would not allow the agents to book tickets on United's competitors, the marketing value of the convenient terminal proved indispensable. SABRE, PARS, and DATAS were soon released to travel agents as well. Following airline deregulation in 1978, an efficient CRS proved particularly important; by some counts, Texas Air executive Frank Lorenzo purchased money-losing Eastern Air Lines specifically to gain control of its SystemOne CRS.

Also in 1976 Videcom international with British Airways, British Caledonian and CCL launched Travicom, the world's first multi-access reservations system (wholly based on Videcom technology), forming a network providing distribution for initially two and subsequently 49 subscribing international airlines (including British Airways, British Caledonian, TWA, Pan American World Airways, Qantas, Singapore Airlines, Air France, Lufthansa, SAS, Air Canada, KLM, Alitalia, Cathay Pacific and JAL) to thousands of travel agents in the UK. It allowed agents and airlines to communicate via a common distribution language and network, handling 97% of UK airline business trade bookings by 1987. The system went on to be replicated by Videcom in other areas of the world including the Middle East (DMARS), New Zealand, Kuwait (KMARS), Ireland, Caribbean, United States and Hong Kong. Travicom was a trading name for Travel Automation Services Ltd. When BA (who by then owned 100% of Travel Automation Services Ltd) chose to participate in the development of the Galileo system Travicom changed its trading name to Galileo UK and a migration process was put in place to move agencies from Travicom to Galileo.

European airlines also began to invest in the field in the 1980s initially by deploying their own reservation systems in their homeland, propelled by growth in demand for travel as well as technological advances which allowed GDSes to offer ever-increasing services and searching power. In 1987, a consortium led by Air France and West Germany's Lufthansa developed Amadeus, modeled on SystemOne. Amadeus Global Travel Distribution was launched in 1992. In 1990, Delta, Northwest Airlines, and Trans World Airlines formed Worldspan, and in 1993, another consortium (including British Airways, KLM, and United Airlines, among others) formed the competing company Galileo International based on Apollo. Numerous smaller companies such as KIU have also formed, aimed at niche markets not catered for by the four largest networks, including the low-cost carrier segment, and small and medium size domestic and regional airlines.

Trends

For many years the GDSs had a dominant position in the travel industry. To bypass the GDS, and avoid high GDS fees, airlines have started to distribute flights directly from their websites. Another possibility to bypass the GDSs is direct connection to travel agencies. American Airlines' direct connect is a prominent example of this development.

Online Hotel Reservations

Online hotel reservations are a popular method for booking hotel rooms. Travelers can book rooms on a computer by using online security to protect their privacy and financial information and by using several online travel agents to compare prices and facilities at different hotels.

Prior to the Internet, travelers could write, telephone the hotel directly, or use a travel agent to make a reservation. Nowadays, online travel agents have pictures of hotels and rooms, information on prices and deals, and even information on local resorts. Many also allow reviews of the traveler to be recorded with the online travel agent.

Online hotel reservations are also helpful for making last minute travel arrangements. Hotels may drop the price of a room if some rooms are still available. There are several websites that specialize in searches for deals on rooms.

Connections to Air Travel

Large hotel chains typically have direct connections to the airline national distribution systems (GDS) (Sabre, Galileo, Amadeus, and Worldspan). These in turn provide hotel information directly to the hundreds of thousands of travel agents that align themselves with one of these systems. Individual hotels and small hotel chains often cannot afford the expense of these direct connections and turn to other companies to provide the connections.

Large-scale Travel Sites

Several large online travel sites are, in effect, travel agencies. These sites send the hotels' information and rates downstream to literally thousands of online travel sites, most of which act as travel agents. They can then receive commission payments from the hotels for any business booked on their websites.

Individual Hotel Websites

An increasing number of hotels are building their own websites to allow them to market their hotels directly to consumers. Non-franchise chain hotels require a "booking engine" application to be attached to their website to permit people to book rooms in real time. One advantage of booking with the hotel directly is the use of the hotel's full cancellation policy as well as not needing a deposit in most situations.

The online booking engine applications are supported by Content management system(CMS).

Database Systems

To improve the likelihood of filling rooms, hotels tend to use several of the above systems. The content on many hotel reservation systems is becoming increasingly similar as more hotels sign up to all the sites. Companies thus have to either rely on specially negotiated rates with the hotels and hotel chains or trust in the influence of search engine rankings to draw in customers.

Mobile Ticketing

Mobile ticketing is the process whereby customers can order, pay for, obtain and/or validate tickets using mobile phones, without the need of a physical ticket. A mobile ticket contains a unique ticket verification (QR code). Mobile tickets reduce the production and distribution costs connected with traditional paper-based ticketing channels and increase customer convenience by providing new and simple ways to purchase tickets. People will not worry about losing a ticket or realizing left tickets at home when arrive at the venue. Mobile tickets are also a way to combat scalping and ticket fraud that has been a big problem for the entertainment industry.

Mobile tickets should not be confused with E-Tickets (electronic tickets) which are used by airlines since 1994, they can be sent by e-mail, printed and shown at the check-in desk at the airport to obtain a boarding pass.

Many train and bus operators in Europe have created phone apps in which tickets can be bought and stored. These include but are not limited to SJ, DSB, NSB, DB and selected local transit authorities.

The first mobile ticketing deployment for a public transport operator in the UK was for Chiltern Railways in 2007. The first transit agency in the US to deploy mobile ticketing was in 2012 with Boston's MBTA and the first agency in Australia was in 2017 with Adelaide Metro.

Philips and Sony developed near field communication (NFC) in 2002. It is build on the same basis as common contactless smartcards. Philips published an early paper on NFC in 2004. In 2004, the NFC Forum was established. NFC incorporated in a mobile phone allows all kind of novel contactless applications, mobile ticketing being an important one of them. Mobile Tickets can be purchased via internet and will be downloaded in a few seconds to the mobile phone, be it in an sms with a 2-D barcode or to the connected NFC chip. In case of NFC at entrance the phone just has to be touched to the scanning device (in fact it makes contact within 10 cm). The GSM Association, GSMA, published a whitepaper on M-Ticketing in 2011. It describes extensively the use and advantages of M-Ticketing, principally the use of NFC technology. They state that NFC is the best technology but "it is expected however that M-Ticketing services using SMS and Bar Code implementations will be prevalent until the point that a critical mass of NFC enabled handsets is available."

Barcode and visual validation is still the accepted way to enable mobile ticketing with proven adoption thanks to the fact that tickets work across all smartphones.

Audio Tour

An audio tour or audio guide provides a recorded spoken commentary, normally through a handheld device, to a visitor attraction such as a museum. They are also available for self-guided tours of outdoor locations, or as a part of an organised tour. It provides background, context, and information on the things being viewed. Audio guides are often in multilingual versions and can be made available in different ways. Some of the more elaborate tours may include original music and interviews. Traditionally rented on the spot, more recently downloaded from the Internet or available via the mobile phone network. Some audio guides are free or included in the entrance fee, others have to be purchased separately.

Electronic Multimedia Guides

Audio guide set for Louvre tour supporting Korean language.

A multimedia electronic guide is a device specially designed to provide audio, visual or textual content to museum visitors with or without user interaction. It may also provide alternative content corresponding to different personal preferences. It may include accessories such as headphones, a digital pen and displays with LEDs or LCD screens.

These smart guides may be operated to supply content in different languages and accents, with different voice alternatives, with text, and with age group specific content. They can be operated in several ways:

- Touch/push-button systems are operated by the visitor. The visitor enters the code assigned to the object or location to the electronic museum guide and the related content is provided.
- Location aware systems operate semi-automatically. They sense the location by several alternative technologies and provide the related content. If the sensing area is not narrow enough to detect every different object then the visitor will enter or select the content he or she wants. Location aware systems provides better quality tours to disabled people.
- Line of Sight Aware Systems operate automatically. They sense the location and the target object and provides the related content. These systems may include software that will attempt to measure the visitor's aims and interest areas and may provide shallower or deeper information for the object. These systems may need special technologies for target detection.

These electronic guides can provide the museum management with useful statistics and reports, which may include tour statistics, visitor statistics, opinions, and other surveys.

Cell Phone Tours

A cell phone tour is an audio tour where pre-recorded or stream audio interpretation for a heritage site or a cultural exhibit is provided via a cell phone. Cell phone audio tours have the advantage that most visitors already have the equipment needed to take the audio tour, being their cell phones.

Each venue is assigned a phone number with appropriate stop numbers, displayed next the exhibit. Once a visitor has dialed in, they will be prompted and can enter the corresponding stop number of the exhibit they're viewing, to hear the recorded content. These tours also enable the visitors to: fast forward, rewind, pause, as well as leave a feedback message for each exhibit or the whole tour; simply by pressing a number. In addition to audio content, some providers are also able to stream video, and text message recent visitors with updates. This is the old-style approach, not used widely.

Smartphone Tours

Smartphones have significant advantages over cell phones, as they have story-triggering technologies (GPS, bluetooth, NFC, QR-code scanner) and can use the power of mobile apps to deliver the right story in the right language in the right place and in the right context (e.g. the evening tour, or a winter tour). Stories could be adjusted to the pace and mood of the user. Of course, such guided tours will use other types of content, above audio: photo, texts, video, quests. Such apps can work online and offline.

Smartphone tours could guide the user outdoor (streets, highways, zoos, parks, archaeological sites) and indoor (museums), using different guiding techniques.

There are many apps available on the market, developed by cities, museums and private companies:

Platform Solutions

Like it happens with any other type of content (e.g. Youtube in video), development of smartphone guiding apps inevitably led to the launch of so-called "platforms", which aggregate thousands of tours and stories:

The Museum Market Changes:

- Museums can publish guided tours in an hour and change it at any moment. The audio guide is not anymore a one-time-off project.
- Museums finally own the content they develop (in the age of hardware audio guides museums rarely owned the content).
- Museums can go outside and provide tours for the city.
- Museums can cooperate with other cultural institutions.
- Museums can invite people form the local communities to help them to develop stories (i.e. leverage the crowdsourcing).

- Museums can finally invade the tourism market and carry on their educational mission on tourists.
- With a new voice, with other museums, with crowdsourced projects, with co-operation with tourism and universities, museums can apply for large grants from public funds.

The Tourism Market Changes:

- Cities can control the tourists traffic, e.g., send tourists away from the city center.
- From the other side, the small cities around big ones can get some tourists by providing guided tours.
- Cities can enrich the rent-a-bike/boat/car experience with storytelling.
- Cities may help tourists to "feel like local" with the help of local communities.
- In the city context, museums and story developers can enjoy local businesses to promote their tours and stories for free, as such tours bring extra value for the users of such businesses. E.g. public transport, mobile operators, hotels, rental services are happy to promote the tours in the vicinity. It is called the Storytelling Smart City concept.

The Modern Technology Implications:

- Self driving cars introduce an opportunity to make mobile storytelling a part of car infotainment system. Passengers will get stories on the roads (presumably for free).
- Personal assistant apps like Apple Siri or Google Assistant will use location based stories as well. Being the audio-based apps, such assistants do need audio based and location based content. Development of "storytelling capacity" for Voice Assistants will be a powerful driver for raising public interest to Mobile Storytelling and attract more storytellers and funds.

Virtual Tour

A virtual tour is a simulation of an existing location, usually composed of a sequence of videos or still images. It may also use other multimedia elements such as sound effects, music, narration, and text. It is distinguished from the use of live television to affect tele-tourism.

The phrase "virtual tour" is often used to describe a variety of videos and photographic-based media. Panorama indicates an unbroken view, since a panorama can be either a series of photographs or panning video footage. However, the phrases "panoramic tour" and "virtual tour" have mostly been associated with virtual tours created using still cameras. Such virtual tours are made up of a number of shots taken from a single vantage point. The camera and lens are rotated around what is referred to as a no parallax point (the exact point at the back of the lens where the light converges).

A video tour is a full motion video of a location. Unlike the virtual tour's static wrap-around feel, a video tour is a linear walk-through of a location. Using a video camera, the location is filmed at a walking pace while moving continuously from one point to another throughout the subject location. 3D virtual tours can be created using 3D reconstruction.

Video-based

With the expansion of video on the internet, video-based virtual tours are growing in popularity. Video cameras are used to pan and walk-through real subject properties. The benefit of this method is that the point of view is constantly changing throughout a pan. However, capturing high-quality video requires significantly more technical skill and equipment than taking digital still pictures. Video also eliminates viewer control of the tour. Therefore, the tour is the same for all viewers and subject matter is chosen by the videographer. Editing digital video requires proficiency with video editing software and has higher computer hardware requirements. Also, displaying video over the internet requires more bandwidth. Due to these difficulties, the task of creating video-based tours is often left to professionals.

Recently different groups have been using Google's system to provide access to private areas, which were previously unavailable to the general public.

Applications

Virtual tours are used extensively for universities and in the real estate and hospitality industries. Virtual tours can allow a user to view an environment while on-line. Currently a variety of industries use such technology to help market their services and product. Over the last few years the quality and accessibility of virtual tours has improved considerably, with some websites allowing the user to navigate the tours by clicking on maps or integrated floor plans.

Web-based or Online

For most business purposes, a virtual tour must be accessible from everywhere. The major solution is a web-based virtual tour. In addition, a rich and useful virtual tour is not just a series of panoramic pictures. A better experience can be obtained by viewing a variety of materials such as that obtained from videos, texts, and still pictures in an interactive web content. There are many ways to gather data in a mixed web content, such as using rich content builders (Java applet or Adobe Flash being two examples) or a Web content management system.

Flash-based tours are becoming very popular today. A study done by the PEW Research Group showed that more than 5 million Americans watched virtual tours every day in 2004. PEW's research data which showed that Americans watching virtual tours rose from 54 million people in 2004 to 72 million people by August 2006, a two-year increase of 18 million.

Thanks in part to the recent explosion of many Internet devices, such as Apple's iPad, iPhone and other tablet computing platforms powered entirely by Google's Android 3 operating systems such as Motorola's Xoom, it can be predicted that consumption of virtual tour content, through the use of Adobe Flash and HTML5/CSS3 driven virtual tours will only increase over time.

Historic Preservation

3D virtual tour technology has been increasingly used in the documentation and preservation of historic properties that are at risk of being razed or undergoing restricted public access. 3D virtual models using standard file formats, such as the Object file (.obj) format, can be stored in digital archives for future academic research and exploration.

Hospitality

Virtual tours are also popular in the hospitality industry. Hotels are increasingly offering online tours on their websites, ranging from "360" stitched photos to professionally produced video tours. These tours are typically offered by hotels in an effort to increase booking revenue by providing online viewers with an immersive view of the property and its amenities.

Virtual Walks

Virtual walk videos are documentary motion pictures shot as the camera continuously moves forward through an urban or natural area. The effect is to allow viewers to experience the sights they would see and the sounds they would hear were they actually traveling along a particular route at the same pace as the camera. Virtual walks based on real-world photography typically do not require the use of virtual reality goggles or headsets of the kind used by gamers.

In realistically simulating the experience of moving through space, virtual walks — or virtual runs or bicycle rides — differ from conventional travel videos, which typically consist of a sequence of mostly static camera setups along a particular route or within a given area. The advantage of the conventional travel video is that one or more narrators or on-screen guides can provide insights into the geographical, historical, political, military, cultural, geological, or architectural aspects of the area.

Virtual walks appeal to those who want to experience the sights and sounds of particular places in the country or the world, but who may not have the time or the financial or physical resources to actually travel there. They also appeal to treadmill or elliptical trainer users, for whom walking or running while watching these videos enhances the reality of the experience (and, at a minimum, reduce the boredom of the exercise).

Some feature-length narrative motion pictures have made use of the virtual walk technique for dramatic purposes. These include the opening sequences of Orson Welles' *Touch of Evil* and Robert Altman's *The Player*, the famous tracking shot through the Copacabana in Martin Scorcese's *Goodfellas*, Alexander Sokurov's *Russian Ark* (which consists of a single 96-minute Steadicam take), and, more recently Alfonso Cuarón's long tracking shots in *Gravity*, and almost the entire narrative structure of Alejandro Gonzáles Iñárrito's *Birdman*.

Global Distribution System

A global distribution system is a computer network, which empowers service providers in the travel industry to carry out seamless transactions. In particular, a GDS is often used by a travel agency, in order to see real-time information and data about the availability of hotel rooms, flights and other travel services.

Using that information, travel agents can then sell travel products and services to their clients.

Benefits of the Hotel using a GDS

Although those in operating in hotel management aim to maximise the number of direct bookings they attract, using a global distribution system helps to reach a larger number of customers. This is because the GDS provides a single point of access for thousands of travel agents across the globe, who can then book hotel rooms for their customers.

Furthermore, a GDS can be especially beneficial for a hotel aiming to attract business or corporate travellers. This is because a large number of organisations still turn to a travel agent to book business travel, rather than attempting to book directly, as it can be easier for them to manage expenses this way.

Costs of using a Global Distribution System

While there are numerous benefits of using a GDS, it comes at a cost too. Standard practice is that a hotel will pay a small initialisation fee, followed by transaction and/or agent fees on every booking that is made. These fees can vary significantly, but it is not unusual for the fees to account for around 10 percent of the amount paid.

For hotel owners, it is important to balance room rates with this in mind. Ideally, to optimise revenue, a hotel should keep room rates low enough to maintain a good relationship with travel agents, but should also ensure they never drop low enough for the payment of transaction or agent fees to become too problematic.

Example:

Hotels can turn to a number of different GDS systems around the world, with each one having its own unique features and target markets. However, it is generally accepted that there is a 'big three' within this industry, which are responsible for the vast majority of travel agency bookings.

Amadeus GDS

When looking at market share for global distribution systems, Amadeus GDS ranks as the market leader and it is estimated that somewhere in the region of 40 percent of all travel agency bookings using GDS systems go through this particular network. However, most of these bookings are linked to flights, rather than hotel rooms.

Nonetheless, Amadeus can provide the hotel industry with excellent access to the European market, in particular, as its database is hosted in Germany and its company headquarters is situated in Germany.

Sabre GDS

The Sabre global distribution system is the closest competitor for Amadeus when it comes to total market share, and it is actually more proportionally reliant on the hotel industry than Amadeus is. In total, it is estimated that more than 200,000 hotels use the network to connect with travel agencies.

The company itself is situated in the U.S. state of Texas, and is comparatively stronger in the North American market than its rivals. Sabre also offers a number of hotel technology solutions.

Travelport GDS

Finally, Travelport is a company that owns the Worldspan, Galileo and Apollo systems. While the parent company is based in the United Kingdom, the Worldspan and Galileo GDS databases are situated in the United States. As an organisation, it provides GDS services and a variety of other travel industry solutions.

One thing to note about Travelport is that it offers access to diverse markets, including those in the Americas, Asia and Europe. Galileo is slightly more popular with hotels, as Worldspan is more closely associated with airlines.

Connecting the Hotel to all Global Distribution Networks

For the most part, hotels connect to GDS networks via a GDS provider. Such a provider will function as an intermediary between the hotel and the global distribution system, and in most cases a GDS provider will actually connect the hotel to all of the three major GDS systems at once, rather than focusing on a single one.

Moreover, a typical GDS provider will also have links to at least one property management system (PMS) or Hotel Channel Manager. All of this means that hotels have the ability to manage their hotel description, room listings, photos and other information across different GDS systems from a single place, while usage can also be automated.

When optimising revenue, a hotel may prefer to attract as many direct bookings as possible, but a global distribution system can be essential for increasing demand and reaching a wider audience. While fees will usually need to be paid to the GDS and the travel agent, room rates can usually be adjusted to ensure all parties benefit financially.

References

- How-airline-e-tickets-work, destinations-travel-guide: adventure.howstuffworks.com, Retrieved 25 August, 2019
- Hegemann, Hendrik (March 2015). “Constructions of Effectiveness and the Rationalization of Counterterrorism Policy: The Case of Biometric Passports”. Studies in Conflict & Terrorism. 38 (3): 199–218. doi:10.1080/1057610X.2014.982384
- Bartneck, Christopher; Masuoka, Aya; Takahashi, Toru; Fukaya, Takugo (2007). An Electronic Museum Guide In Use. Psychology of Aesthetics, Creativity, and the Arts. 1. pp. 53–55. CiteSeerX 10.1.1.67.3278. doi:10.1037/1931-3896.1.2.114. ISBN 978-0-7695-2385-9
- Global-distribution-system: revfine.com, Retrieved 26 June, 2019

Permissions

All chapters in this book are published with permission under the Creative Commons Attribution Share Alike License or equivalent. Every chapter published in this book has been scrutinized by our experts. Their significance has been extensively debated. The topics covered herein carry significant information for a comprehensive understanding. They may even be implemented as practical applications or may be referred to as a beginning point for further studies.

We would like to thank the editorial team for lending their expertise to make the book truly unique. They have played a crucial role in the development of this book. Without their invaluable contributions this book wouldn't have been possible. They have made vital efforts to compile up to date information on the varied aspects of this subject to make this book a valuable addition to the collection of many professionals and students.

This book was conceptualized with the vision of imparting up-to-date and integrated information in this field. To ensure the same, a matchless editorial board was set up. Every individual on the board went through rigorous rounds of assessment to prove their worth. After which they invested a large part of their time researching and compiling the most relevant data for our readers.

The editorial board has been involved in producing this book since its inception. They have spent rigorous hours researching and exploring the diverse topics which have resulted in the successful publishing of this book. They have passed on their knowledge of decades through this book. To expedite this challenging task, the publisher supported the team at every step. A small team of assistant editors was also appointed to further simplify the editing procedure and attain best results for the readers.

Apart from the editorial board, the designing team has also invested a significant amount of their time in understanding the subject and creating the most relevant covers. They scrutinized every image to scout for the most suitable representation of the subject and create an appropriate cover for the book.

The publishing team has been an ardent support to the editorial, designing and production team. Their endless efforts to recruit the best for this project, has resulted in the accomplishment of this book. They are a veteran in the field of academics and their pool of knowledge is as vast as their experience in printing. Their expertise and guidance has proved useful at every step. Their uncompromising quality standards have made this book an exceptional effort. Their encouragement from time to time has been an inspiration for everyone.

The publisher and the editorial board hope that this book will prove to be a valuable piece of knowledge for students, practitioners and scholars across the globe.

Index

Q

R

S

T

U

V

W

CPSIA information can be obtained
at www.ICGtesting.com
Printed in the USA
LVHW060904030122
707669LV00002B/349

9 781647 283759